Jean Ingelow

**Fated to be free**

Jean Ingelow

**Fated to be free**

ISBN/EAN: 9783337281960

Printed in Europe, USA, Canada, Australia, Japan

Cover: Foto ©Lupo / pixelio.de

More available books at **www.hansebooks.com**

By JEAN INGELOW
AUTHOR OF "OFF THE SKELLIGS," ETC. ETC.

THREE VOLS.—II.

LONDON
TINSLEY BROTHERS, CATHERINE STREET
STRAND
1875

# CONTENTS OF VOL. II.

| CHAPTER | PAGE |
|---|---|
| I. EMILY | 1 |
| II. THE AMERICAN GUEST | 21 |
| III. WEARING THE WILLOW | 41 |
| IV. AN EASY DISMISSAL | 60 |
| V. A MORNING CALL | 76 |
| VI. MR. MORTIMER GOES THROUGH THE TURNPIKE | 99 |
| VII. THE RIVER | 124 |
| VIII. THE DEAD FATHER ENTREATS | 143 |
| IX. SOPHISTRY | 169 |
| X. DANTE AND OTHERS | 193 |
| XI. SELF-WONDER AND SELF-SCORN | 214 |
| XII. THAT RAINY SUNDAY | 236 |

# CHAPTER I.

### EMILY.

> "Not warp'd by passion, awed by rumour,
>   Not grave through pride, nor gay through folly,
> An equal mixture of good humour,
>   And sensible, soft melancholy.
>
> "'Has she no faults then,' Envy says, 'Sir?'
>   'Yes, she has one, I must aver;
> When all the world conspires to praise her
>   The woman's deaf, and does not hear.'"

JOHN MORTIMER was sitting at breakfast the very morning after this conversation had taken place at Melcombe. No less than four of his children were waiting on him; Gladys was drying his limp newspaper at a bright fire, Barbara spreading butter on his toast, little Hugh kneeling on a chair, with his elbows on the table, was reading him a choice anecdote from a child's book of natural history, and Anastasia, while he poured out his coffee with one hand, had got hold of the other, which she was folding up industriously in her pinafore and frock, because she said it was cold. It was a windy, chilly, and exasperatingly bright spring morning; the sunshine appeared to prick the traveller all over rather than to warm him. Not at all the morning for an early walk, but John, lifting up his eyes, saw a lady in the garden, and in another instant Mrs. Frederic Walker was shown in.

"What, Emily!" exclaimed John, starting up.

"Yes, John; but my soldier and my valuable infant are both quite well. Now, if you don't go on with your breakfast, I shall depart. Let me sit by the fire and warm my feet."

"You have breakfasted?"

"Of course. How patriarchal you look, John, sitting in state to be adored!"

Thereupon, turning away from the fire, she began to smile upon the little Anastasia, and without any more direct invitation, the small coquette allowed herself to be decoyed from her father to sit on the visitor's knee. Emily had already thrown off her fur wraps, and the child, making herself very much at home in her arms, began presently to look at her brooch and other ornaments, the touch of her small fingers appearing to give pleasure to Emily, who took up one of the fat little pink hands, and kissed it fondly.

"What is that lady's name, Nancy?" said John.

"Mrs. Nemily," answered the child.

"You have still a little nursery English left about you, John," said Emily. "How sweet it is! My boy has that yet to come; he can hardly say half-a-dozen words."

Then Gladys entering the room with a cup and saucer, she rose and came to the table.

"That milk looks so nice—give me some of it. How pleasant it is to feel cold and hungry, as one does in England! No, John, not ham; I will have some bread and marmalade. Do the children always wait on you, John, at breakfast?"

There was something peculiarly sweet and penetrative in the voices of Brandon and his sister; but this second quality sometimes appeared to give more significance to their words than they had intended.

"Always. Does it appear an odd arrangement in your eyes?"

"Father," said Barbara, "here is your paper. I have cut the leaves."

"Thank you, my dear; put it down. You should

consider, Emily, my great age and exaltation in the eyes of these youngsters. Don't you perceive that I am a middle-aged man, madam?"

"Middle-aged, indeed! You are not thirty-six till the end of September, you know—the 28th of September. And oh, John, you cannot think how young you look! just as if you had stolen all these children, and they were not really yours. You have so many of them, too, while I have only one, and he such a little one—he is only two years old."

While she spoke a bell began to ring, and the two elder children, wishing her good-bye, left the room.

"Do you think those girls are growing like their mother?" asked John.

"I think they are a little. Perhaps that pretty way they have of taking up their eye-glasses when they come forward to look at anything, makes them seem more like than they are."

John scarcely ever mentioned his wife, but before Emily most people spoke without much reserve.

"Only one of the whole tribe is like her in mind and disposition," he continued.

"And that's a good thing," thought Emily, but she did not betray her thought.

While this talk went on the two younger children had got possession of Mrs. Nemily's watch (which hung from her neck by a long Trichinopoly chain), and were listening to a chime that it played. Emily took the boy on her knee, and it did not appear that he considered himself too big to be nursed, but began to examine the watch, putting it to his ear, while he composedly rested his head on her shoulder.

"Poor little folk," thought John, "how naturally they take to the caresses of a young mother!"

Another bell then rang.

"What order is kept in your house!" said Emily, as both the children departed, one with a kiss on her dimpled cheek and the other on his little scratched fist, which already told of much climbing.

"That is the school-room bell," John answered; and then Mrs. Frederic Walker laughed, and said, with a look half whimsical, half wistful—

"Oh, John, you're going to be so cross?"

"Are you going to make me cross? You had better tell me at once, then, what you are come for. Has Giles returned?"

"He came in late last night. I know what he

went for, John. He thought it best to tell me. He is now gone on to the station about some affairs of his own. It seems that you both took Joey Swan's part, and were displeased with that Laura."

"Of course. She made the poor fellow very miserable for a long time. Besides, I am ashamed of the whole derogatory affair. Did Giles see that she burnt those letters—foolish, cold-hearted creature?"

"'Foolish,' I dare say; but 'cold-hearted,' I don't know. St. George declared to me that he thought she was as much in love now as that goose Joseph ever was."

"Amazing!" exclaimed John, very much discomfited.

"And she tried hard to make him promise that he would keep the whole thing a profound secret, especially from you; and so of course he declined, for he felt that you must be the proper person to tell it to, though we do not know why. He reasoned with her, but he could make nothing of her."

"Perhaps she wants to bring it on again," said John. "What a pity he returned the letters before Joe had sailed!"

"No, it was the right thing to do. And, John, if love is really the sacred, strong, immortal passion made out by all the poets and novelists, I cannot see, somehow, that putty ought to stand in its light. It ought to have a soul above putty."

"With all my heart," said John; "but you see in this case it hadn't."

"It would be an *astonishingly* disadvantageous thing for our family if she ran away and married him just now, when Valentine has been making himself so ridiculous. But there is no doubt we could bring it on again, and have it done if we chose," said Emily.

John looked at her with surprise.

"But then," she continued, "I should say that the man ought to be thought of as well as herself, and she might prove a thoroughly unsuitable, foolish wife, who would soon tire of him. SHE might be very miserable also. She would not have half the chance of happiness that an ordinary marriage gives. And, again, Santo Domingo is notoriously unhealthy. She might die, and if we had caused the marriage, we should feel that."

"Are you addressing this remarkable speech to yourself or to *the chair?*" said John, laughing.

"To the chair. But, if I am the meeting, don't propose as a resolution that this meeting is *tête montée*. John, you used to say of me before I married that I was troubled with intuitions."

"I remember that I did."

"You meant that I sometimes saw consequences very clearly, and felt that the only way to be at peace was to do the right thing, having taken some real trouble to find out what it was."

"I was not aware that I meant that. But proceed."

"When Laura was here in the autumn she often talked to Liz about little Peter Melcombe's health, and said she believed that his illness at Venice had very much shaken his constitution. His mother, she said, never would allow that there had been much the matter with him, though she had felt frightened at the time. It was the heat, Laura thought, that had been too much for him. Now, you know if that poor little fellow were to die, Valentine, who has nothing to live on, and nothing to do, is his heir. What a fine thing it would be for him!"

"I don't see yet what you mean."

"Mrs. Melcombe found out before Giles left Melcombe all about these letters. She came into the room, and Laura, who seems to have been filled with a ridiculous sort of elation to think that somebody had really loved her, betrayed it in her manner, and between her and Giles it was confessed. Mrs. Melcombe was very wroth."

"Laura has a right to do as she pleases," said John; "no one can prevent it."

"She has the right, but not the power. WE can do as we please, or we can let Mrs. Melcombe do as SHE pleases."

"You mean that we can tell my gardener's son that my cousin (whom he no longer cares for) is in love with him, and, by our assistance and persuasion, we can, if we choose, bring on as foolish a marriage as ever was contemplated, and one as disadvantageous to ourselves. Now for the alternative. What can it be?"

"Mrs. Melcombe can take Laura on the Continent again, and she proposed to do it forthwith."

"And leave her boy at school? A very good thing for him."

"No, she means to take him also, and not come back till Joseph is at the other end of the world."

"Two months will see him there."

"Well, John, now you have stated the case, it does seem a strange fancy of mine to wish to interfere, and if to interfere could possibly be to our advantage——"

"You would not have thought of it! No, I am sure of that. Now my advice is, that we let them alone all round. I don't believe, in the first place, that Joe Swan, now he has change, freedom, and a rise in life before him, would willingly marry Laura if he might. I am not at all sure that, if it came to the point, she would willingly marry him at such short notice, and leave every friend she has in the world. I think she would shrink back, for she can know nothing worth mentioning of him. As to the boy, how do you know that a tour may not be a very fine thing for him? It must be better than moping at Melcombe under petticoat government; and even if Joe married Laura to-morrow, we could not prevent Mrs. Melcombe from taking him on the Continent whenever she chose."

Emily was silent.

"And what made you talk of a runaway match?" continued John.

"Because she told Giles that the last time she saw Joseph he proposed to her to sneak away, get married before a magistrate, and go off without saying a word to anybody."

"Fools," exclaimed John, "both of them! No, we cannot afford to have any runaway matches—and of such a sort too! I should certainly interfere if I thought there was any danger of that."

"I hope you would. He wanted her to propose some scheme. I think scorn of all scheming. If she had really meant to marry him, his part should have been to see that she did it in a way that would not make it worse for her afterwards. He should have told Mrs. Melcombe fairly that she could not prevent it, and he should have taken her to church and married her like a man before plenty of witnesses in the place where she is known. If he had not shown such a craven spirit, I almost think I would have taken his part. Now, John, I know what you think; but I should have felt just the same if Valentine had not made himself ridiculous, and if I was quite sure that this would not end in a runaway match after all, and the *True Blue* be full of it."

"I believe you," said John; "and I always had a great respect for you, 'Mrs. Nemily.'"

"What are you laughing at, then?"

"Perhaps at the matronly dignity with which you have been laying down the law."

"Is that all? Oh, I always do that now I am married, John."

"You don't say so! Well, Joe Swan has worked hard at improving himself; but though good has come out of it in the end for him, it is certainly a very queer affair. Why, in the name of common sense, couldn't Laura be contented with somebody in her own sphere?"

"I should like to know why Laura was so anxious the matter should be concealed from you," said Emily.

"Most likely she remembers that Swan is in my employment, or she may also be 'troubled with intuitions,' and know by intuition what I think of her."

"And how is Aunt Christie?" asked Emily, after a little more talk concerning Joseph's affairs.

"Well and happy; I do not believe it falls to the lot of any old woman to be happier in this *oblate spheroid*. The manner in which she acts dragon over Miss C. is a joy to me, the only observer. She always manages that we shall never meet excepting in her presence; when I go into the schoolroom to read prayers, I invariably find her there before me. She insists, also, on presiding at all the schoolroom meals. How she found out the state of things here I cannot tell, but I thankfully let her alone. I never go out to smoke a cigar in the evening, and notice a stately female form stepping forth also, but Aunt Christie is sure to come briskly stumping in her wake, ready to join either her or me."

"You don't mean to imply anything?"

"Of course not! but you yourself, before you married, were often known to take my arm at flower-shows, &c., in order to escape from certain poor fellows who sighed in vain."

"Yes, you were good about that; and you remind me of it, no doubt, in order to claim the like friendliness from me now the tables are turned. John, the next time I take your arm in public it will be to extend my matronly countenance to those modest efforts of yours at escaping attention, for you know yourself to be quite unworthy of notice!"

"Just so; you express my precise feeling."

"It is a pity you and Grand are so rich!"

"Why? You do not insinuate, I hope, that I and my seven are merely eligible on that account! Now, what are you looking at me for, with that little twist in your lips that always means mischief?"

"Because I like you, and I am afraid you are being spoilt, John. I do so wish you had a nice wife. I should, at least, if you wished it yourself."

"A saving clause! Have you and Fred discussed me, madam?"

"No, I declare that we have not."

"I hope you have nobody to recommend, because I won't have her! I always particularly disliked red hair."

"Now what makes you suppose I was thinking of any one who has red hair?"

"You best know yourself whether you were *not*."

"Well," said Emily, after a pause for reflection, "now you mention it (I never did), I do not see that you could do better."

"I often think so myself, and that is partly why I am so set against it! No, Emily, it would be a shame to joke about an excellent and pleasant woman. The fact is, I have not the remotest intention of ever marrying again at all."

"Very well," said Emily, "it is not my affair; it was your own notion entirely that I wanted to help you to a wife."

And she sat a moment cogitating, and thinking that the lady of the golden head had probably lost her chance by showing too openly that she was ready.

"What are you looking at?" said John. "At the paths worn in my carpets? That's because all the rooms are thoroughfares. Only fancy any woman marrying a poor fellow whose carpets get into that state every three or four years."

"Oh," said Emily, "if that was likely to stand in your light, I could soon show you how to provide a remedy."

"But my father hates the thoughts of bricks and mortar," said John, amused at her seriousness, "and I inherit that feeling."

"John, the north front of your house is very ugly. You have five French windows on a line—one in each of these rooms, one in the hall; you would only have to run a narrow passage-like conservatory in front of them, enter it by the hall window, and each room by its own window, put a few plants in the conservatory, and the thing is done in a fortnight. Every room has its back window; you would get into the back garden as you do now; you need not touch the back of the house, that is all smothered in vines and creepers, as you are smothered in children!"

"The matter shall have my gravest consideration," said John, "provided you never mention matrimony to me again as long as you live."

"Very well," said Emily, "I promise; but there is St. George coming. I must not forget to tell you that I saw Joseph this morning at a distance; he was standing in the lea of the pigstye, and cogitating in the real moony style."

"It was about his outfit," exclaimed John; "depend upon it it was not about Laura."

And so the colloquy ended, and John walked down his own garden, opened the wicket that led to his gardener's cottage, and saw Joseph idly picking out a weed here and there, while he watched the bees, some of whom, deluded by the sunshine, had come forth, and were feebly hanging about the opening of the hive.

"Joe," said John, with perfect decision and directness, "I have a favour to ask of you."

Joseph was startled at first; but as no more was said, he presently answered, "Well, sir, you and yours have done me so many, that I didn't ought to hesitate about saying I'll grant it, whatever it is."

"If you should think of marrying before you go——"

"Which I don't, sir," interrupted the young man rather hastily.

"Very good; then if you change your mind, I want your promise that you will immediately let me know."

"Yes, sir," said Joseph, as if the promise cost him nothing, and suggested nothing to his mind, "I will."

"There," thought John, as he turned away, "he does not know what he is about; but if she brings the thing on again, I believe he will keep faith with me, and a clandestine marriage I am determined shall not be."

He then went into the town and found, to his surprise, that Brandon had already seen his father, and had told him that Dorothea Graham had engaged herself to him. John was very much pleased, but his father treated the matter with a degree of apathy which rather startled and disturbed him.

Old Augustus was in general deeply interested in a marriage; he had helped several people to marry, and whether he approved or disapproved of any one in particular, he was almost sure, when he had been lately told of it, to make some remarks on the sacredness of the institution, and on the advantages of an early marriage for young men.

He, however, said nothing, though Brandon was one of his chief favourites; but having just related the fact, took up the *Times*, and John opened his letters, one of them being from his son Johnny, written in a fully-formed and beautiful hand, which made its abrupt style and boyish vehemence the more observable.

"MY DEAREST FATHER,—It's all right. Mr. —— took me to Harrow, and Dr. B. examined me, and he said—oh, he said a good deal about my Latin verses, and the books I'm *in*, but I can't tell you it, because it seems so muffish. And, papa, I wish I might bring Crayshaw home for the Easter holidays; you very nearly promised I should; but I wanted to tell you what fun I and the other fellows had at the boat-race. You can hardly think how jolly it was. I suppose when I get into the great school I shall never see it. We ran down shouting and yelling after the boats. I thought I should never be happy again if Cambridge didn't win. It was such a disgustingly sleety, blowy, snowy, windy, raspy, muddy day, as you never saw. And such crowds of fellows cheering and screeching out to the crews. Such a rout!

> 'The Lord Mayor lent the City P'lice,
> The cads ran down by scores and scores
> With shouting roughs, and scented muffs,
> While blue were flounces, frills, and gores.
> On swampy meads, in sleeted hush,
> The swarms of London made a rush,
> And all the world was in the slush.'

Etcetera. That's part of Crayshaw's last; it's a parody of one of those American fogies. Dear father, you will let me come home, won't you; because I do assure you I shall get in with the greatest ease, even if I'm not coached for a day more. A great many fellows here haven't a tutor at all.—I remain, your affectionate son,

"A. J. MORTIMER.

" P.S.—Will you tell Gladys that my three puppies, which she says are growing nicely, are not, on any account, to be given away; and will you say that Swan is not to drown them, or do anything with them, till I've chosen one, and then he may sell the others. And I hope my nails and screws and my tools have not been meddled with. The children are not to take my things. It often makes me miserable to think that they get my nails and my paddle when I'm gone."

John Mortimer smiled, and felt rather inclined to let the boy come home, when, looking up, he observed that his father was dozing over the newspaper, and that he shivered.

Master Augustus John did not get an answer so soon as he had hoped for it, and when it came it was dated from a little, quiet place at the seaside, and let him know that his grandfather was very poorly, very much out of sorts, and that his father had felt uneasy about him. Johnny was informed that he must try to be happy, spending the Easter holidays at his tutor's. His grandfather sent him a very handsome "tip," and a letter written in such a shaky hand, that the boy was a good deal impressed, and locked it up in his desk, lest he should never have another.

## CHAPTER II.

### THE AMERICAN GUEST.

"Shall we rouse the night-owl with a catch that will draw three souls out of one weaver?"

IN less than a week from the receipt of his son's letter, John Mortimer wrote again, and gave the boy leave to come home, but on no account to bring young Crayshaw with him, if a journey was likely to do him harm.

Johnny accordingly set off instantly (the holidays having just begun), and, travelling all night, reached the paternal homestead by eight o'clock in the morning.

His father was away, but he was received with rapture by his brothers and sisters. His little brothers admired him with the humble reverence of small boys for big ones, and the girls delighted in his school-boy slang, and thought themselves honoured by his companionship.

Crayshaw was an American by birth, but his elder

brother (under whose guardianship he was) had left him in England as his best chance of living to manhood, for he had very bad health, and the climate of his native place did not suit him.

Young Gifford Crayshaw had a general invitation to spend the holidays at Brandon's house, for his brother and Brandon were intimate friends; but boys being dull alone, Johnny Mortimer and he contrived at these times to meet rather often, sometimes to play, sometimes to fight—even the latter is far better than being without companionship, more natural, and on the whole more cheerful.

"And I'm sure," said Aunt Christie, when she heard he was coming, "I should never care about the mischief he leads the little ones into when he's well, if he could breathe like other people when he's ill; you may hear him half over the house when he has his asthma."

Crayshaw came by the express train in the afternoon, and was met by the young Mortimers in the close carriage. He was nearly fifteen, and a strange contrast to Johnny, whose perfect health, ardent joyousness, and lumbering proportions never were so observable as beside the clear-cut face of the other, the slow gait, an expression of countenance at once audacious, keen, and sweet, together with that peculiar shadow under the eyelids which some people consider to betoken an early death.

Crayshaw was happily quite well that afternoon, and accordingly very noisy doings went on; Miss Crampton was away for her short Easter holiday, and Aunt Christie did not interfere if she could help it when Johnny was at home.

That night Master Augustus John Mortimer, his friend, and all the family were early asleep; not so the next. It was some time past one o'clock A.M. when John Mortimer and Brandon, who had been dining together at a neighbour's house, one having left his father rather better, and the other having come home from the Isle of Wight, walked up towards the house deep in conversation, till John, lifting up his eyes, saw lights in the schoolroom windows. This deluded father calmly remarked that the children had forgotten to put the lamp out when they went to bed. Brandon thought he heard a sound uncommonly like infant revelry, but he said nothing, and the two proceeded into the closed house, and went softly up-stairs.

"Roast pork," said Brandon, "if ever I smelt that article in my life!"

They opened the schoolroom door, and John beheld, to his extreme surprise, a table spread, his eldest son at the head of it, his twin daughters, those paragons of good behaviour, peeling potatoes, and the other children, all more or less dishevelled, sitting round, blushing and discomfited.

"My dears!" exclaimed John Mortimer, "this I never could have believed of you! One o'clock in the morning!"

Perfect silence. Brandon thought John would find it beneath his dignity to make a joke of this breach of discipline. He was rather vexed that he should have helped to discover it, and feeling a little *de trop*, he advanced to the top of the table. "John," he said with a resigned air and with a melancholy cadence in his voice that greatly impressed the children.

"Come," thought John as he paused, "they deserve a 'wigging,' but I don't want to make a 'Star-chamber matter' of this. I wish he would not be so supernaturally serious."

"John," repeated Brandon, "on occasion of this

unexpected hospitality, I feel called upon to make a speech."

John sat down, wondering what would come next.

"John, ladies and gentlemen," said Brandon, "when I look around me on these varied attractions, when I behold those raspberry turnovers of a flakiness and a puffiness so ethereal, that one might think the very eyes of the observer should drop lightly on them, lest that too appreciative glance should flatten them down—I say, ladies and gentlemen, when I smell that crackling, when I cast my eyes on those cinders in the gravy, I am irresistibly reminded of occasions when I myself, arrayed in a holland pinafore, have presided over like entertainments; and of one in particular when, being of tender age—of one occasion, I say, that is never to be forgotten, when, during the small hours of the night, I was hauled out of bed to assist in mixing hardbake, by one very dear to us all—who shall be nameless."

What more he would have added will never be known, for with ringing laughter that spoke for the excellence of their lungs, the whole tableful of young Mortimers, with the exception of Johnnie, rose, and, as if by one impulse, fell upon their father.

"Hold hard," he was heard to shout, "don't smother me." But he received a kissing and hugging of great severity; the elder ones who had understood Brandon's speech, closing him in; the little ones, who only perceived to their delight that the occasion had become festive again, hovering round, and getting at him where they could. So that when they parted, and he was visible again, sitting radiant in the midst of them, his agreeable face was very red, and he was breathing fast and audibly. "I'll pay you for this!" he exclaimed, when he observed, to his amusement, that Brandon's serious look was now really genuine, as if he was afraid the experiment might be repeated on himself. "Johnnie, my boy, shake hands, I forgive you this once. And you may pass the bottle." Johnnie, who knew himself to be the real offender, made haste to obey. "It's not blacking, of course," continued John, looking at the thick liquor with distrust.

"The betht black currant," exclaimed his heir, "at thirteen-penth a bottle."

"And where's Cray?" exclaimed John, suddenly observing the absence of his young guest.

"He's down in the kitchen, dishing up the pudding," said Barbara blushing, and she darted out of the room, and presently returned, other footsteps following hers.

"Cray," exclaimed John, as the boy seemed inclined to linger outside, "don't stand there in the draught. And so it is not by your virtuous inclinations that you have hitherto been excluded from this festive scene?"

"No, sir," said Crayshaw with farcical meekness of voice and air, "quite the contrary. It was that I've met with a serious accident. I've been run over."

John looked aghast. "You surely have not been into the loose-box," he said anxiously.

"Oh no, father, nothing of the sort," said Barbara. "It was only that he was down in the kitchen on his knees, and two blackbeetles ran over his legs. You should never believe a word he says, father."

"But that was the reason the pudding came to grief," continued Crayshaw; "they were very large and fierce, and in my terror I let it fall, and it was squashed. When I saw their friends coming on to fall upon it, I was just about to cry, 'Take it all, but spare my life!' when Barbara came and rescued me. I hope," he went on, yet more meekly, "I hope it was not an unholy self-love that prompted me to prefer my life to the pudding!"

The children laughed, as they generally did when Crayshaw spoke, but it was more at his manner than at his words. And now, peace being restored, everybody helped everybody else to the delicacies, John discreetly refraining from any inquiry as to whether this was the first midnight feast over which his son had presided, but he could not forbear to say, "I suppose your grandfather's 'tip' is to blame for this?"

"If everybody was like the Grand," remarked Crayshaw, "Tennyson never need have said—

> 'Vex not thou the schoolboy's soul
> With thy shabby *tip*.'"

"Now, Cray," said Brandon, "don't you emulate Valentine's abominable trick of quoting."

"And I have often begged you two not to parody the Immortals," said John. "The small fry you may make fun of, if you please, but let the great alone."

"But he ithn't dead," reasoned Master Augustus

John; "I don't call any of thoth fellowth immortal till they're dead."

"It's a very bad habit," continued his father.

"And he's made me almost as bad as himself," observed Crayshaw in the softest and mildest of tones. "Miss Christie said this very morning that there was no bearing me, and I never did it till I knew him. I used to be so good, everybody loved me."

John laughed, but was determined to say his say.

"You never can take real pleasure again in any poetry that you have mauled in that manner. Miss Crampton was seriously annoyed when she found that you had altered the girl's songs, and made them ridiculous."

The last time, in fact, that Johnnie and Crayshaw had been together, they had deprived themselves of their natural rest in order to carry out these changes; and the first time Miss Crampton gave a music lesson after their departure, she opened the book at one of their improved versions, which ran as follows :—

> "Wink to me only with thy nose,
> And I will sing through mine."

Miss Crampton hated boyish vulgarity; she turned

the page, but matters were no better. The two youths had next been at work on a song in which a muff of a man, who offers nothing particular in return, requests 'Nancy' to gang wi' him, leaving her home, her dinner, her brooches, her best gowns, &c., behind, to walk through snow-drifts, blasts, and other perils by his side, and afterwards strew flowers on his clay. Desirous as it seemed to show that the young person was not so misguided as her silence has hitherto left the world to think, they had added a verse, which ran as follows:—

> "'Ah, wilt thou thus, for his loved sake,
>  All manner of hardships dare to know?'
> The fair one smiled whenas he spake,
>  And promptly answered, 'No, sir; no.'"

"Cray," said John Mortimer, observing the boy's wan appearance, "how could you think of sitting up so late?"

"Why, the thupper wath on purpoth for him," exclaimed Johnnie. "We gave it in hith honour, ath a mark of thympathy."

"Because he was burnt out," said Gladys. "Papa, did you know? his tutor's house was burnt down, and the boys had to escape in the night."

"But it wath a great lark," observed Johnnie, "and he knowth he thought tho."

"Yes," said Crayshaw, folding his hands with farcical mock meekness, "but I saved hardly anything — nothing whatever, in fact, but my Yankee accent, and that only by taking it between my teeth."

"There was not enough of it to be worth saving, my dear boy," said Brandon.

Crayshaw's face for once assumed a genuine expression, one of alarm. He was distinguished at school for the splendid Yankee dialect he could put on, as Johnnie was for his mastery of a powerful Devonshire lingo; but if scarcely a hint of his birthplace remained in his daily speech, and he had not noticed any change, there was surely danger lest this interesting accomplishment should be declining also.

"I am always imitating the talk I hear in the cottages," he remarked; "I may have lost it so."

"Perhaps, as Cray goes to so many places, it may get scattered about," said little Bertram; but he was speedily checked by Johnnie, who observed with severity that they didn't want any "thrimp thauth."

"He mutht thimmer," said Johnnie, "thath what

he mutht do. He mutht be thrown into an iron pot, with a gallon of therry cobbler, and a pumpkin pie, and thome baked beanth, and a copy of the Biglow Paperth, and a handful of thalt, and they mutht all thimmer together till he geth properly flavoured again."

"Wouldn't it be safer if he was only dipped in?" asked the same "shrimp" who had spoken before.

As this was the second time he had taken this awful liberty, he would probably have been dismissed the assembly but for the presence of his father. As it was, Johnnie and Crayshaw both looked at him, not fiercely but steadily, whereupon the little fellow with deep blushes slid gently from his chair under the table.

A few days after this midnight repast, Emily, knowing that John Mortimer was away a good deal, and having a perfectly gratuitous notion that his children must be dull in consequence, got Valentine to drive her over one morning to invite them to spend a day at Brandon's house.

A great noise of shouting, drumming on battledores, and blowing through discordant horns, let them know, as they came up the lane, that the community was in a state of high activity; and when they reached the garden gate they were just in time to see the whole family vanish round a corner, running at full speed after a donkey on which Johnnie was riding.

The visitors drove inside the gate, and waited five minutes, when the donkey, having made the circuit of the premises, came galloping up, the whole tribe of young Mortimers after him. They received Emily with loving cordiality, and accounted for the violent exercise they had been taking by the declaration that this donkey never would go at all, unless he heard a great noise and clatter at his heels.

"So that if Johnnie wanted to go far, as far as to London," observed one of the panting family, "it would be awkward, wouldn't it?"

"And he's only a second-hand donkey, either," exclaimed little Janie in deep disparagement of the beast; "father bought him of the blacksmith."

"But isn't it good fun to see him go so fast?" cried another. "Would you like to see our donkey do it again?"

"And see him 'witch the world with noble ass-manship,'" said Valentine.

Whereupon a voice above said rather faintly, "Hear, hear!" and Crayshaw appeared leaning out of a first-floor window, the pathetic shadow more than commonly evident in his eyes, in spite of a mischievous smile. He had but lately recovered from a rheumatic fever, and was further held down by frequent attacks of asthma. Yet the moment one of these went off, the elastic spirits of boyhood enabled him to fling it into the background of his thoughts, and having rested awhile, as he was then doing, he became, according to the account Gladys gave of him at that moment, "just like other boys, only ten times more so!"

Emily now alighted, and as they closed about her and hemmed her in, donkey and all, she felt inclined to move her elbows gently, as she had sometimes seen John do, in order to clear a little space about him. "Why does not Cray come down, too?" she asked.

"I think he has had enough of the beast," said Barbara, "for yesterday he was trying to make him jump; but the donkey and Cray could not agree about it. He would not jump, and at last he pitched Cray over his head."

"Odd," said Valentine; "that seems a double contradiction to the proverb that 'great wits jump.'" Valentine loved to move off the scene, leaving a joke with his company. He now drove away, and Johnnie informed Emily that he had already been hard at work that morning.

"I've a right to enjoy mythelf after it," he added, looking round in a patronising manner, "and I have. I've not had a better lark, in fact, since Grand was a little boy."

By these kind, though preposterous words, the assembly was stimulated to action. The frightful clatter, drumming, and blowing of horns began again, and the donkey set off with all his might, the Mortimers after him. When he returned, little Bertram was seated on his back. "Johnnie and Cray have something very particular to do," she was informed with gravity.

"For their holiday task?"

"Oh no, for that lovely electrifying machine of cousin Val's. Cray is always writing verses; he is going to be a poet. Johnnie was saying last week that it was not at all hard to turn poetry into Latin, and Val said he should have the machine if he could translate some that Cray wrote the other day. Do you think the Romans had any buttons and buttonholes?"

"I don't know. Why?"

"Because there are buttons in one of the poems. Cray says it is a tribute—a tribute to this donkey that father has just given us. He was inspired to write it when he saw him hanging his head over the yard gate."

Thereupon the verses, copied in a large childish hand, were produced and read aloud:—

### A TRIBUTE.

> The jackass brayed;
> And all his passionate dream was in that sound
> Which, to the stables round
> And other tenements, told of packs that weighed
> On his brown haunches; also that, alas
> His true heart sighed for Jenny, that fair ass
> Who backward still and forward paced
> With panniers and the curate's children graced.
> Then, when she took no heed, but turned aside
> Her head, he shook his ears
> As much as to say "Great are—as these—my fears."
> And while I wept to think how love that preyed
> On the deep heart not worth a button seemed
> To her for whom he dreamed;
> And while the red sun stained the welkin wide,
> And summer lightnings on the horizon played,
> Again the jackass brayed.

"And here's the other," said Gladys. "Johnnie

says it would be much the easier to do, only he is doubtful about the 'choker.'"

### THE SCHOOLBOY TO HIS DRESS SUIT.

Nice is broiled salmon, whitebait's also nice
  With bread and butter served, no shaving thinner.
*Entrées* are good; but what is even ice—
  Cream ice—to him that's made to dress for dinner?
Oh my dress boots, my studs, and my white tie
  Termed choker (emblem of this heart's pure aim),
Why are good things to eat your meed? Oh why
  Must swallow-tails be donned for tasting game?
The deep heart questions vainly,—not for ease
  Or joy were such invented;—but this know,
I'd rather dine off hunks of bread and cheese
  Than feast in state rigged out in my dress clo'.
                                        G. C.

Emily, after duly admiring these verses, gave her invitation, and it was accepted with delight. Nothing, they said, could be more convenient. Father had told them how Mr. Brandon was having the long wing of the house pulled down, the part where cousin Val's room used to be; so he had been obliged to turn out his nests, and his magic lantern, and many other things that he had when he was a little boy.

"And he says we shall inherit them."

"And when father saw him sitting on a heap of bricks among his things, he says it put him in mind of Marius on the ruins of Carthage."

"So now we can fetch them all away."

Emily then departed, after stipulating that the two

little ones, her favourites, should come also. "Darlings!" she exclaimed, when she saw their stout little legs so actively running to ask Miss Christie's leave. "Will my boy ever look at me with such clear earnest eyes? Shall I ever see such a lovely flush on his face, or hear such joyous laughter from him?"

Time was to answer this question for her, and a very momentous month for the whole family began its course. Laura, writing from Paris to Liz, made it evident to those who knew anything of the matter, that Mrs. Melcombe, as she thought, had carried her out of harm's way; and it is a good thing Laura did not know with what perfect composure and ambitious hope Joseph made his preparations for the voyage. The sudden change of circumstances and occupation, and the new language he had to learn, woke him thoroughly from his dream, and though it had been for some long time both deep and strong, yet it was to him now as other dreams "when one awaketh;" and Laura herself, now that she had been brought face to face, not with her lover, but with facts, was much more reasonable than before. Brandon had said to her pointedly, in the presence of her sister-in-law, "If you and this young man had decided to marry, no law, human or divine, could have forbidden it." But at the same time Amelia had said, "Laura, you know very well that though you love to make romances about him, you would not give up one of the comforts of life for his sake."

Laura, in fact, had scarcely believed in the young man's love till she had been informed that it was over. She longed to be sought more than she cared to be won; it soothed and comforted what had been a painful sense of disadvantage to know that one man at least had sighed for her in vain. He would not have been a desirable husband, but as a former lover she could feign him what she pleased, and while, under new and advantageous circumstances, he became more and more like what she feigned, it was not surprising that in the end she forgot her feigning, and found her feet entangled for good and all in the toils she herself had spread for them.

In the meantime Johnnie and Crayshaw, together with the younger Mortimers, did much as they liked, till Harrow school reopened, when the two boys returned, departing a few hours earlier than was necessary that they might avoid Miss Crampton, a functionary whom Johnny held in great abhorrence.

At the same period Grand suddenly rallied, and, becoming as well as ever, his son, who had made many journeys backwards and forwards to see him, brought him home, buying at the railway station, as he stepped into his father's carriage, the *Times* and the *Wigfield Advertiser and True Blue*, in each of which he saw a piece of news that concerned himself, though it was told with a difference.

In the *Times* was the marriage of Giles Brandon, Esq., &c., to Dorothea, elder daughter of Edward Graham, Esq.; and in the local paper, with an introduction in the true fustian style of mock concealment, came the same announcement, followed by a sufficiently droll and malicious account of the terrible inconvenience another member of this family had suffered a short time since by being snowed up, in which state he still continued, as snow in that part of the world had forgotten how to melt.

A good deal that was likely to mortify Valentine followed this, but it was no more than he deserved.

John laughed. "Well, Giles is a dear fellow," he said, throwing down the paper. "I am pleased at his marriage, and they must submit to be laughed at like other people."

## CHAPTER III.

### WEARING THE WILLOW.

> "My Lord Sebastian,
> The truth you speak doth lack some gentleness
> And time to speak it in; you rub the sore
> When you should bring the plaster."
> *The Tempest.*

WHEN John Mortimer reached the banking-house next morning, he found Valentine waiting for him in his private sitting-room.

"I thought my uncle would hardly be coming so early, John," he said, "and that perhaps you would spare me a few minutes to talk things over."

"To be sure," said John, and looking more directly at Valentine, he noticed an air of depression and gloom which seemed rather too deep to be laid to the account of the *True Blue*.

He was stooping as he sat, and slightly swinging his hat by the brim between his knees. He had reddened at first, with a sullen and half-defiant expression, but this soon faded, and, biting his lips, he brought himself with evident effort to say—

"Well, John, I've done for myself, you see; Giles has married her. Serves me right, quite right. I've nothing to say against it."

"No, I devoutly hope you have not," exclaimed John, to whom the unlucky situation became evident in an instant.

"Grand always has done me the justice to take my part as regards my conduct about this hateful second engagement. He always knew that I would have married poor Lucy if they would have let me—married her and made the best of my frightful, shameful mistake. But as you know, Mrs. Nelson, Lucy's mother, made me return her letters a month ago, and said it must be broken off, unless I would let it go dragging on and on for two years at least, and that was impossible, you know, John, because—because, I so soon found out what I'd done."

"Wait a minute, my dear fellow," John interrupted hastily, "you have said nothing yet but what expresses very natural feelings. I remark, in reply, that your regret at what you have long seen to be unworthy conduct need no longer disturb you on the lady's account, she having now married somebody else."

"Yes," said Valentine, sighing restlessly.

"And," John went on, looking intently at him, " on your own account I think you need not at all regret that you had no chance of going and humbly offering yourself to her again, for I feel certain that she would have considered it insulting her to suppose she could possibly overlook such a slight. Let me speak plainly, and say that she could have regarded such a thing in no other light."

Then, giving him time to think over these words, which evidently impressed him, John presently went on, " It would be ridiculous, however, now, for Dorothea to resent your former conduct, or St. George either. Of course they will be quite friendly towards you, and you may depend upon it that all this will very soon appear as natural as possible; you'll soon forget your former relation towards your brother's wife; in fact you must."

Valentine was silent awhile, but when he did speak he said, "You feel sure, then, that she would have thought such a thing an insult?" He meant, you feel sure, then, that I should have had no chance even if my brother had not come forward.

" Perfectly sure," answered John with confidence.

"That was a step which, from the hour you made it, you never could have retraced."

Here there was another silence; then—

"Well, John, if you think so," said the poor fellow—"this was rather a sudden blow to me, though."

John pitied him; he had made a great fool of himself, and he was smarting for it keenly. His handsome young face was very pale, but John was helping him to recollect his better self, and he knew it. "I shall not allude to this any more," he continued.

"I'm very glad to hear you say so," said John.

"I came partly to say — to tell you that now I am better, quite well, in fact, I cannot live at home any longer. At home! Well, I meant in St. George's house, any longer."

The additional knowledge John had that minute acquired of the state of Valentine's feeling, or what he supposed himself to feel, gave more than usual confidence and cordiality to his answer.

"Of course not. You will be considering now what you mean to do, and my father and I must help you. In the first place there is that two thousand pounds; you have never had a shilling of it yet. My father was speaking of that yesterday."

"Oh," answered Valentine, with evident relief, and with rather a bitter smile, "I thought he proposed to give me that as a wedding present, and if so, goodness knows I never expect to touch a farthing of it."

"That's as hereafter may be," said John, leading him away from the dangerous subject. Valentine began every sentence with a restless sigh.

"I never chose to mention it," he remarked. "I had no right to consider it as anything else, nor did I."

"He does not regard it in any such light," said John. "He had left it to you in his will, but decided afterwards to give it now. You know he talks of his death, dear old man, as composedly as of to-morrow morning. He was reminding me of this money the other day when he was unwell, and saying that, married or unmarried, you should have it made over to you."

"I'm very deeply, deeply obliged to him," said Valentine, with a fervour that was almost emotion. "It seems, John, as if that would help me,—might get me out of the scrape, for I really did not know where to turn. I've got nothing to do, and had nothing to live on, and I'm two and twenty."

"Yes."

"I do feel as if I was altogether in such an ignominious position."

As John quite agreed with him in this view of his position, he remained silent.

Valentine went on, "First, my going to Cambridge came to nothing on account of my health. Then a month ago, as I didn't want to go and live out in New Zealand by myself, couldn't in fact, the New Zealand place was transferred to Liz, and she and Dick are to go to it, Giles saying that he would give me a thousand pounds instead of it. I shall not take that, of course."

"Because he will want his income for himself," John interrupted.

Valentine proceeding, "And now since I left off learning to farm,—for that's no use here,—I've got nothing on earth to do."

"Have you thought of anything yet?"

"Yes."

"Well, out with it."

"John," remarked Valentine, as the shadow of a smile flitted across John's face, "you always seem to me to know what a fellow is thinking of! Perhaps you would not like such a thing,—wouldn't have it?"

John observed that he was getting a little less gloomy as he proceeded.

"But whether or not, that two thousand pounds will help me to some career, certainly, and entirely save me from what I could not bear to think of, *her* knowing that I was dependent on Giles, and despising me for it."

"Pooh," exclaimed John, a little chafed at his talking in this way, "what is St. George's wife likely to know, or to care, as to how her brother-in-law derives his income? But I quite agree with you that you have no business to be dependent on Giles; he has done a great deal for his sisters, he should now have his income for himself."

"Yes," said Valentine.

"You have always been a wonderfully united family," observed John pointedly; "there is every reason why that state of things should continue."

"Yes," repeated Valentine, receiving the covert lecture resignedly.

"And there is no earthly end, good or bad, to be served," continued John, "by the showing of irritation or gloom on your part, because your brother has chosen to take for himself what you had previously and with all deliberation thrown away."

"I suppose not, John," said Valentine quite humbly.

"Then what can you be thinking of?"

"I don't know."

"You have not talked to any one as you have done to me this morning?"

"No, certainly not."

"Well, then, decide while the game is in your own hand that you never will."

So far from being irritated or sulky at the wigging that John was bestowing on him, Valentine was decidedly the better for it. The colour returned to his face, he sat upright in his chair, and then he got up and stood on the rug, as if John's energy had roused him, and opened his eyes also, to his true position.

"You don't want to cover yourself with ridicule, do you?" continued John, seeing his advantage. "Why, even if you cared to take neither reason, nor duty, nor honour into the question, surely the only way to save your own dignity from utter extinction is to be, or at least seem to be, quite indifferent as to what the lady may have chosen to do, but very glad that your brother should have taken a step which makes it only fair to you that he and his wife should forget your former conduct."

"John," said Valentine, "I acknowledge that you are right."

John had spoken quite as much, indeed more, in Brandon's interest than in Valentine's. The manner in which the elder had suffered the younger to make himself agreeable and engage himself to Dorothea Graham, and how, when he believed she loved him, he had made it possible for them to marry, were partly known to him and partly surmised. And now it seemed in mockery of everything that was decent, becoming, and fair that the one who had forsaken her should represent himself as having waked, after a short delusion, and discovered that he loved her still, letting his brother know this, and perhaps all the world. Such would be a painful and humiliating position also for the bride. It might even affect the happiness of the newly-married pair; but John did not wish to hint at these graver views of the subject; he was afraid to give them too much importance, and he confidently reckoned on Valentine's volatile disposition to stand his friend, and soon enable him to get over his attachment. All that seemed wanting was some degree of present discretion.

"John, I acknowledge that you are right," repeated Valentine, after an interval of thought.

"You acknowledge—now we have probed this subject and got to the bottom of it—that it demands of you absolute silence, and at first some discretion?"

"Yes; that is settled."

"You mean to take my view?"

"Yes, I do."

As he stood some time lost in thought, John let him alone and began to write, till, thinking he had pondered enough, he looked up and alluded to the business Valentine had come about.

"You may as well tell it me, unless you want to take my father into your council also: he will be here soon."

"No; I thought it would be more right if I spoke to you first, John, before my uncle heard of it," said Valentine.

"Because it is likely to concern me longer?" asked John.

"Yes; you see what I mean; I should like, if uncle and you would let me, to go into the bank; I mean as a clerk—nothing more, of course."

"I should want some time to consider that matter," said John. "I was half afraid you would propose this, Val. It's so like you to take the easiest thing that offers."

"Is it on my account or on your own that you shall take time?"

"On both. So far as you are concerned, it is no career to be a banker's clerk."

"No; but, John, though I hardly ever think of it, I cannot always forget that there is only one life between me and Melcombe."

"Very true," said John coolly; "but if it is ill waiting for a dead man's shoes, what must it be waiting for a dead child's shoes?"

"I do not even wish or care to be ever more than a clerk," said Valentine; "but that, I think, would fill up my time pleasantly."

"Between this and what?"

"Between this and the time when I shall have finally decided what I will do. I think eventually I shall go abroad."

John knew by this time that he would very gladly not have Valentine with him, or rather under him; but an almost unfailing instinct, where his father was concerned, assured him that the old man *would* like it.

"Shall I speak to my father about it for you?" he said.

"No, John, by no means, if you do not like it. I would not be so unfair as let him have a hint of it till you have taken the time you said you wanted."

"All right," said John; "but where, in case you became a clerk here, do you propose to live?"

"Dick A'Court lived in lodgings for years," said Valentine, "so does John A'Court now, over the pastrycook's in the High Street."

"And you think you could live over the shoemaker's?"

"Why not?"

"I have often met Dick meekly carrying home small parcels of grocery for himself. I should like to catch you doing anything of the sort!"

"I believe I can do anything now I have learned to leave off quoting. I used to be always doing it, and to please Dorothea I have quite given it up."

"Well," said John, "let that pass."

He knew as well as possible what would be his father's wish, and he meant to let him gratify it. He was a good son, and, as he had everything completely in his own power, he may be said to have been very indulgent to his father, but the old man did not know it any more than he did.

Mr. Augustus Mortimer had a fine house, handsomely appointed and furnished. From time to time, as his son's family had increased, he had added accommodation. There was an obvious nursery; there was an evident schoolroom, perfectly ready for the son, and only waiting, he often thought, till it should be said to his father, "Come up higher."

It was one of John's theories that there should be a certain homely simplicity in the dress, food, and general surroundings of youthful humanity; that it should not have to walk habitually on carpets so rich that little dusty feet must needs do damage, and appear intruders; nor be made to feel all day that somebody was disturbed if somebody else was making himself happy according to his lights, and in his own fashion.

But of late Mr. Augustus Mortimer had begun

to show a degree of infirmity which sometimes made his son uncomfortable that he should have to live alone. To bring those joyous urchins and little, laughing, dancing, playful girls into his house was not to be thought of. What was wanted was some young relative to live with him, who would drive him into the town and home again, dine with him, live in his presence, and make his house cheerful. In short, as John thought the matter over, he perceived that it would be a very good thing for his father to have Valentine as an inmate, and that it would be everything to Valentine to be with his father.

People always seemed to manage comfortable homes for Valentine, and make good arrangements for him, as fast as he brought previous ones to nought.

Very few sons like to bring other people into their fathers' houses, specially in the old age of the latter; but John Mortimer was not only confident of his own supreme influence, but he was more than commonly attached to his father, and had long been made to feel that on his own insight and forethought depended almost all that gave the old man pleasure.

His father seldom disturbed any existing arrangements, though he often found comfort from their being altered for him; so John decided to propose to him to have his brother's son to live with him. In a few days, therefore, he wrote to Valentine that he had made up his mind, and would speak to his father for him, which he did, and saw that the nephew's wish gave decided pleasure; but when he made his other proposal he was quite surprised (well as he knew his father) at the gladness it excited, at those thanks to himself for having thought of such a thing, and at certain little half-expressed hints which seemed intended to meet and answer any future thoughts his son might entertain as to Valentine's obtaining more influence than he would approve. But John was seldom surprised by an after-thought; he was almost always happy enough to have done his thinking beforehand.

He was in the act of writing a letter to Valentine the next morning at his own house, and was there laying the whole plan before him, when he saw him driving rapidly up to the door in the little pony chaise, now the only carriage kept at Brandon's house. He sprang out as if in urgent haste, and burst into the room in a great hurry.

"John," he exclaimed, "can you lend me your

phaeton, or give me a mount as far as the junction? Fred Walker has had one of his attacks, and Emily is in a terrible fright. She wants another opinion: she wishes Dr. Limpsey to be fetched, and she wants Grand to come to her."

This last desire, mentioned as the two hurried together to the stable, showed John that Emily apprehended danger.

Emily's joyous and impassioned nature, though she lived safely, as it were, in the middle of her own sweet world—saw the best of it, made the best of it, and coloured it all, earth and sky, with her tender hopefulness—was often conscious of something yet to come, ready and expectant of *the rest of it*. The rest of life, she meant; the rest of sorrow, love, and feeling.

She had a soul full of unused treasures of emotion, and pure, clear depths of passion that as yet slumbered unstirred. If her heart was a lute, its highest and lowest chords had never been sounded hitherto. This also she was aware of, and she knew what their music would be like when it came.

She had been in her girlhood the chief idol of many hearts; but joyous, straightforward, and full of childlike sweetness, she had looked on all her adorers in such an impartially careless fashion, that not one of them could complain. Then, having confided to John Mortimer's wife that she could get up no enthusiasm for any of them, and thought there could be none of that commodity in her nature, she had at last consented, on great persuasion, to take the man who had loved her all her life, " because he wouldn't go away, and she didn't know what else to do with him; he was such a devoted little fellow, too, and she liked him so much better than either of his brothers ! "

So they were married; Captain Walker was excessively proud and happy in his wife, and Mrs. Walker was as joyous and sweet as ever. She had satisfied the kindly pity which for a long while had made her very uncomfortable on his account ; and, O happy circumstance ! she became in course of time the mother of the most attractive, wonderful, and interesting child ever born. In the eyes, however, of the invidious world, he was uncommonly like his plain sickly father, and not, with that exception, at all distinguished from other children.

John made haste to send Valentine off to the junction, undertook himself to drive his father over to see Emily, and gathered from the short account Valentine gave whilst the horse was put too, that Fred Walker had been taken ill during the night with a fainting fit. He had come from India for his year's leave in a very poor state of health, and with apprehended heart disease. Only ten days previously Emily had persuaded him that it would be well to go to London for advice. But a fainting fit had taken place, and the medical man called in had forbidden this journey for the present. He had appeared to recover, so that there seemed to be no more ground for uneasiness than usual; but this second faintness had lasted long enough to terrify all those about him.

Grand was very fond of his late brother's step-daughter; she had always been his favourite, partly on account of her confiding ease and liking for him, partly because of the fervent religiousness that she had shown from a child.

'The most joyous and gladsome natures are often most keenly alive to impressions of reverence, and wonder, and awe. Emily's mind longed and craved to annex itself to all things fervent, deep, and real. As she walked on the common grass, she thought the better of it because the feet of Christ had trodden it also. There were things which she—as the angels—"desired to look into;" but she wanted also to do the right thing, and to love the doing of it.

With all this half Methodistic fervour, and longing to lie close at the very heart of Christianity, she had by nature a strange fearlessness; her religion, which was full of impassioned loyalty, and her faith, which seemed to fold her in, had elements in them of curiosity and awed expectation, which made death itself appear something grand and happy, quite irrespective of a simply religious reason. It would show her "the rest of it." She could not do long without it; and often in her most joyous hours she felt that the crown of life was death's most grand hereafter.

## CHAPTER IV.

### AN EASY DISMISSAL.

> " Admired Miranda!
> Indeed the top of admiration! worth
> What's dearest to the world."
> *The Tempest.*

"WELL, father, it's too true!"

"You don't say so?"

"Yes; he died, Dr. Mainby's housekeeper says, at five o'clock this morning. The doctor was there all night, and he's now come home, and gone to bed."

"One of the most unfortunate occurrences I ever heard of. Well, that that is, is—and can't be helped. I'd have given something (over and above the ten-and-sixpence) to have had it otherwise; but I 'spose, Jemmy, I 'spose we understand the claims of decency and humanity." It was the editor of the *True Blue* who said this.

"I 'spose we do," answered the son sturdily, though sulkily; "but that's the very best skit that Blank Blank ever did for us."

## AN EASY DISMISSAL.

"Blank Blank" was the signature under which various satirical verses appeared in the *True Blue*.

"Paid for, too—ten-and-six. Well, here goes, Jemmy." He took a paper from his desk, read it over with a half smile. "One or two of the jokes in it will keep," he observed; then, when his son nodded assent, he folded it up and threw it in the fire. This was a righteous action. He never got any thanks for doing it; also a certain severity that he was inclined to feel against the deceased for dying just then, he quickly turned (from a sense of justice) towards the living members of his family, and from them to their party, the "pinks" in general. Then he began to moralise. "Captain Walker—and so he's dead—died at five o'clock this morning. It's very sudden. Why Mrs. Walker was driving him through the town three days ago."

"Yes," answered the son; "but when a man has heart complaint, you never know where you are with him."

A good many people in Wigfield and round it discussed that death during the day; but few, on the whole, in a kindlier spirit than had been displayed by the editor of the opposition paper. Mrs. A' Court, wife of the vicar, and mother of Dick A' Court, remarked that she was the last person to say anything unkind, but she did value consistency.

"Everybody knows that my Dick is a high churchman; they sent for him to administer the holy communion, and he found old Mr. Mortimer there, a layman, who is almost, I consider, a Methodist, he's so low church; and poor Captain Walker was getting him to pray extempore by his bed. Even afterward he wouldn't let him out of his sight. And Dick never remonstrated. Now, that is not what I could have hoped of my son; but when I told him so, he was very much hurt, said the old man was a saint, and he wouldn't interfere. 'Well, my dear,' I said, 'you must do as you please; but remember that your mother values consistency.'"

When Mrs. Melcombe, who, with her son and Laura, was still at Paris, heard of it, she also made a characteristic remark. "Dear me, how sad!" she exclaimed; "and there will be that pretty bride, Mrs. Brandon, in mourning for months, till all her wedding dresses, in fact, are out of fashion."

Mrs. Melcombe had left Melcombe while it was at its loveliest, all the hawthorns in flower, the peonies and lilies of the valley. She chose first to go to Paris, and then when Peter did not seem to grow, was thin and pale, she decided—since he never seemed so well as when he had no lessons to do—that she would let him accompany them on their tour.

Melcombe was therefore shut up again; and the pictures of Daniel Mortimer and the young lieutenant, his uncle, remained all the summer in the dark. But Wigfield House was no sooner opened after Captain Walker's funeral than back came the painters, cleaners, and upholsterers, to every part of it; and the whole place, including the garden, was set in order for the bride.

Emily was not able to have any of the rest and seclusion she so much needed; but almost immediately took her one child and went to stay with her late husband's father till she could decide where to live.

Love that has been received affects the heart which has lost it quite differently from a loss where the love has been bestowed. The remembrance of it warms the heart towards the dear lost donor; but if the recollection of life spent together is without remorse, if, as in Emily's case, the dead man has been wedded as a tribute to his acknowledged love, and if he has not only been allowed to bestow his love in peace without seeing any fault or failing that could give him one twinge of jealousy—if he has been considered, and liked thoroughly, and, in easy affectionate companionship, his wife has walked beside him, delighting him, and pleased to do so—then, when he is gone, comes, as the troubled heart calms itself after the alarms of death and parting, that one, only kind of sorrow which can ever be called with truth " the luxury of grief."

In her mourning weeds, when she reached Fred's father's house, Emily loved to sit with her boy on her lap, and indulge in passionate tears, thinking over how fond poor Fred had been, and how proud of her. There was no sting in her grief, no compunction, for she knew perfectly well how happy she had made him; and there was not the anguish of personal loss, and want, and bereavement.

She looked pale when she reached Mr. Walker's house, but not worn. She liked to tell him the details of his son's short illness; and the affectionate, irascible old man not only liked to hear them, but derived pleasure from seeing this fine young woman, this interesting widow, sitting mourning for his son. So he made much of her, and pushed her sister Louisa at once into the background for her sake.

The sisters having married twin brothers, Mr. Walker's elder sons, neither had looked on himself as heir to the exclusion of the other; but Emily's pale morsel of a child was at once made more important than his father had ever been. Louisa, staying also with her husband in the house, was only the expectant mother of a grandson for him; and the rich old man now began almost immediately to talk of how he should bring up Emily's boy, and what he should do for him—taking for granted, from the first, that his favourite daughter-in-law was to live with him and keep his house.

Louisa took this change in Mr. Walker very wisely and sweetly—did not even resent it, when, in the presence of his living son, he would aggravate himself into lamentations over the dead one, as if in him he had lost his all.

Sometimes he wondered a little himself at this quiescence—at the slight impression he seemed to make on his son, whom he had fully intended to rouse to remonstrance about it—at the tender way in which the young wife ministered to her sister, and at the great change for the worse that he soon began to observe in Emily's appearance.

Nobody liked to tell him the cause, and he would not see it; even when it became an acknowledged fact, which every one else talked of, that the little one was ill, he resolutely refused to see it; said the weather was against a child born in India—blamed the east wind. Even when the family doctor tried to let him know that the child was not likely to be long for this world, he was angry, with all the unreasonable volubility of a man who thinks others are deceiving him, rather than grieved for the peril of the little life and the anguish of the mother's heart.

Now came indeed "the rest of it." What a rending away of heart and life it seemed to let go the object of this absorbing, satisfying love! Now she was to lose, where the love had been bestowed; and she felt as if death itself was in the bitter cup.

It was not till the child was actually passing away, after little more than a fortnight's illness, that his grandfather could be brought to believe in his danger.

He had been heaping promises of what he would do for him on the mother, as if to raise her courage. With kindly wrong-headed obstinacy he had collected and detailed to her accounts of how ill other children had been and had recovered, had been getting fresh medical opinions, and proposing to try new remedies; but no sooner was all over, and the afflicted mother was led from her dead child by his son, than he tormented himself and the doctors by demanding why he had been kept in the dark so long, why he had not been allowed to try change of air, why, if the symptoms showed mortal disease from the first, he had been allowed to set his heart on the child as he had done. No one now had anything to say to Emily. She had only been a widow a month, and the first loss had had no bitterness in it, though she had sorrowed with the tender affection of a loyal heart. The death of her child was almost the loss of all.

Valentine in the meantime had taken his sister Liz to a little quiet place; there, as her marriage could not be put off, and the ship was decided on in which they were to sail for New Zealand, he acted the part of father, and gave her away at the quietest wedding possible, seeing her off afterwards, and returning to take up his abode in his uncle's house, about three weeks after the death of Emily's little child. Not one of the late inhabitants had been left in his old home excepting Mrs. Henfrey, who remained to receive the bride, and was still there, though the newly-married pair had been home a week. Valentine had found ample time to consider how he should behave to Dorothea, Mrs. Brandon. He had also become accustomed to the thought of her being out of his reach, and the little excitement of wonder as to how they should meet was not altogether displeasing to him. "Giles will be inclined, no doubt, to be rather jealous of me," was his thought; "I shall be a bad fellow if I don't take care to show him that there is no need for it. D. must do the same. Of course she will. Sweet D.! Well, it can't be helped now."

It was natural enough that he should cogitate over the best way of managing his first meeting with them; but he had not been an hour in his uncle's house before he found that Grand was shortly going to give a great dinner party for the bride mainly consisting of relatives and very old friends. This, it was evident, would be the most natural time for him to present himself.

Valentine loved comfort and luxury, and finding himself established quite as if he had been a younger son in the house—a horse kept for him to ride, and a small sitting-room set aside in which he could see his friends—he experienced a glow of pleasure at first, and he soon perceived that his presence was a real pleasure to his old uncle; so, settling himself with characteristic ease in his place, he felt hourly more and more content with his new home.

It was not till he came down into the drawing-room before dinner on the day of the party that he began to feel excited and agitated. A good many of the guests were already present, he went up to one and to another, and then advanced to speak to Miss Christie, who was arrayed in a wonderful green gown, bought new for the occasion.

"Mr. and Mrs. Brandon," sounded clearly all down the long room, and he turned slowly and saw them. For one instant they appeared to be standing quite still, and so he often saw them side by side in his thoughts ever after. The bride looked serenely sweet, a delicate blush tinging her face, which was almost of infantine fairness and innocence; then old Grand's white head came in the way as he advanced to meet her and take her hand, bowing low with old-fashioned formality and courtesy. Several other people followed and claimed her acquaintance, so that they were closed in for the moment. Then he felt that now was the time for him to come forward, which he did, and as the others parted again to let Grand take her to a seat, they met face to face.

"Ah, Valentine," she said, so quietly, with such an unexcited air; she gave him her hand for a moment, and it was over. Then he shook hands with his brother, their eyes met, and though both tried hard to be grave, neither could forbear to smile furtively; but Giles was much the more embarrassed of the two.

During dinner, though Valentine talked and laughed, he could not help stealing a minute now and then to gaze at the bride, till John, darting a sudden look at him, brought him to his senses; but he cogitated about her, though he did not repeat the offence. "Is it lilac, or grey, or what, that she has on? That pale stuff must be satin, for it shines. Oh, meant for mourning perhaps. How wonderfully silent Giles is! How quiet they both are!"

This observation he made to himself several times during the evening, catching the words of one and the other whatever part of the room he was in, almost as distinctly as they did themselves; but he only looked once at Dorothea, when something made him feel or think that she had drawn her glove off. His eyes wandered then to her hand. Yes, it was so—there was the wedding ring.

With what difficulty, with what disgrace he had contrived to escape from marrying this young woman! His eyes wandered round the room. Just so she would have looked, and every one else would have looked, if this wedding dinner had been made for *his* bride, but he would not have been sitting up in the corner with three girls about him, laughing and making laugh. No, and he would not have stood rather remote from her, as Giles did. He thought he would have been proudly at her side. Oh, how could he have been such a fool? how could he? how could he?

"She would have loved me just as well, just so she would have lifted up her face, as she does now, and turned towards me."—No! The bride and her husband looked at one another for an instant, and in one beat of the heart he knew not only that no such look had ever been in her eyes for him, but he felt before he had time to reason his conviction down, that in all likelihood there never would have been. Then, when he found that Dorothea seemed scarcely aware of his presence, he determined to return the compliment, got excited, and was the life and soul of the younger part of the company. So that when the guests dispersed, many were the remarks they made about it.

"Well, young Mortimer need not have been quite so determined to show his brother how delighted he was not to be standing in his shoes." "Do you think Brandon married her out of pity?" "She is a sweet young creature. I never saw newly-married people take so little notice of one another. It must have been a trial to her to meet young Mortimer again, for no doubt she was attached to him."

A quarter of an hour after the bride had taken her leave, and when all the other guests were gone, Valentine went into the hall, feeling very angry with himself for having forgotten that, as he was now a member of her host's family, he might with propriety have seen Dorothea into the carriage. "This," he thought, "shall not occur again."

The hall doors were open, servants stood about as if waiting still. He saw a man's figure. Some one, beyond the stream of lamplight which came from the house, stood on the gravel, where through a window he could command a view of the staircase.

It was little past eleven, the moon was up, and as the longest day was at hand, twilight was hardly over, and only one star here and there hung out of the heavens.

"Why, that is Giles," thought Valentine. "Strange! he cannot have sent Dorothea home alone, surely."

Giles approached the steps, and Valentine, following the direction of his eyes, saw a slender figure descending the stairs.

Dorothea! She was divested now of the shimmering satin and all her bridal splendour. How sweet and girlish she looked in this more simple array! Evidently they were going to walk home through the woods and lanes, see glow-worms and smell the hedge roses. For an instant Valentine was on the point of proposing to accompany them part of the way, but recollected himself just in time to withdraw into the shadow made by a stand of greenhouse plants, and from thence see Giles come up the steps, take the delicate ungloved hand and lay it on his arm, while the hall doors were closed behind them.

Adam and Eve were returning to Paradise on foot. The world was quite a new world. They wanted to see what it was like by moonlight, now they were married.

Valentine walked disconsolately up the stairs, and there at the head of them, through a wide-open door, he saw a maid. The pale splendours of Dorothea's gown were lying over her arm, and she was putting gold and pearls into a case. He darted past as quickly as he could, so glad to get out of sight, lest she should recognise him, for he shrewdly suspected that this was the same person who had been sent with Dorothea to Wigfield, when she first went there—one Mrs. Brand. So, in fact, it was; her husband was dead, she no longer sailed in old Captain Rollin's yacht, and Brandon had invited her to come and stay in the house a while, and see her young lady again.

How glad he was to get away and shelter himself in his own room!—an uncomfortable sensation this for a fine young man. "What should I have done but for Grand and John?" was his thought. Grand and John were very considerate the next day. In the first place, Grand scarcely mentioned the bride during breakfast; in fact, so far as appeared, he had forgotten the party altogether. John was also considerate, gave Valentine plenty to do, and in a way that made him feel the yoke, took him in hand and saw that he did it.

It is often a great comfort to be well governed. John had a talent for government, and under his dominion Valentine had the pleasure of feeling, for the first time in his life, that he had certain things to do which must and should be done, after which he had a full right to occupy himself as he pleased.

## CHAPTER V.

### A MORNING CALL.

> "Learn now for all
> That I, which know my heart, do here pronounce
> By the very truth of it, I care not for you."—*Cymbeline.*

"JOHN," said Valentine, ten days after this dinner party, "you have not called on D. yet, nor have I."

"No," John answered, observing his wish, "and it might not be a bad plan for us to go together."

"Thank you, and if you would add the twins to—to make the thing easier and less formal."

"Nonsense," said John; "but yes, I'll take some of the children, for of course you feel awkward." He did not add, "You should not have made such a fool of yourself," lest Valentine should answer, "I devoutly wish I had not;" but he went on, "And why don't you say Dorothea, instead of using a nickname?"

"I always used to call her D.," said Valentine.

"All the more reason why you should not now," answered John.

And Valentine murmured to himself—

"'These strong Egyptian fetters I must break, or lose myself in dotage' (*Antony and Cleopatra*)." This he added from old habit. "I'll quote everything I can think of to D., just to make her think I have forgotten her wish that I should leave off quoting; and if that is not doing my duty by St. George, I should like to know what is. Only that might put it into his head to quote too, and perhaps he might have the best of it. I fancy I hear him saying, 'Art thou learned?' I, as William, answer, 'No, sir.' 'Then learn this of me,' he makes reply, 'to have is to have; for all your writers do consent that *ipse* is he. Now you are not *ipse*, for I am he. He, sir, that hath married this woman. Therefore, you clown, abandon, which is—,' &c., &c. What a fool I am!"

John, adding the twins and little Bertram to the party, drove over on a Saturday afternoon, finding no one at home but Mrs. Henfrey.

"St. George," she said, "has taken to regular work, and sits at his desk all the morning, and for an hour or two in the afternoon, excepting on Saturday, when he gives himself a half-holiday, as if he was a school-boy."

"And where was he now?" John asked.

"Somewhere about the place with Dorothea; he had been grubbing up the roots of the trees in a corner of the little wood at all leisure times; he thought of turning it into a vegetable garden."

"Why, we always had more vegetables than we could use," exclaimed Valentine, "and we were three times as large a family."

"Very true, my dear, but they are full of schemes —going to grow some vegetables, I think, and flowers, for one of the county hospitals. It would not be like him, you know, to go on as other people do."

"No," Valentine answered. "And he always loved a little hard work out of doors; he is wise to take it now, or he would soon get tired of stopping peaceably at home, playing Benedict in this dull place."

The children were then sent out to find where the young wife was, and come and report to their father, telling her that he would pay his call out of doors.

"And so you are still here, sister," observed Valentine, willing to change the subject, for he had been rather disconcerted by a quiet smile with which she had heard his last speech.

"Yes, my dear, the fact is, they won't let me go."

"Ah, indeed?"

"Of course I never thought they would want me. And the morning after they came home I mentioned that I had been looking out for a house—that small house that I consulted John about, and, in fact, took."

Mrs. Henfrey was hardly ever known to launch into narration. She almost always broke up her remarks by appeals to one and another of her listeners, and she now did not go on till John had made the admission that she had consulted him. She then proceeded with all deliberation—

"But you should have seen how vexed St. George looked. He had no idea, he said, that I should ever think of leaving him; and, indeed, I may mention to you in confidence, both of you, that he always drew for me what money I said was wanted for the bills, and he no more thought of looking at my housekeeping books than my father did."

"Really," said Valentine.

He was quite aware of this, to him, insignificant

fact, but to have said more would only have put her out, and he wanted her to talk just then.

"And so," she continued slowly, "I said to him, I said, 'My dear Giles, I have had a pleasant home in this house, many, many years, indeed, ever since you were a child; but it is my opinion (and you will find it is the general opinion) that every young wife should have her house to herself.' I did not doubt at all that this was her opinion too, only I considered that as he had spoken so plainly, she might not like to say so."

"No, very likely not," said John, when she stopped, as if stranded, till somebody helped her on with a remark.

"You are quite right, John, any one might have thought so; but in a minute or two. 'Well,' said St. George, 'this is rather a blow;' and what does that pretty creature do but come and sit by me, and begin to coax me. 'She wanted me so much, and it would be so kind if I would but stop and do as I always had done, and she would be so careful to please me, and she had always thought the house was so beautifully managed, and everything in such order, and so regular.'"

"So it is," Valentine put in. "She is quite right there."

"'And she didn't know how to order the dinner,' she said; and so she went on, till I said, 'Well, my dears, I don't wish that there should be any mistake about this for want of a little plain speaking.'"

"Well?" said John, when she came to a dead stop.

"And she said, 'You love St. George, don't you, just as much as if he was related to you?' 'How can any one help loving him?' 'And I know if you leave us he won't be half so comfortable. And nobody should ever interfere with you.' So I said I would keep their house for them, and you may suppose how glad I was to say it, for I'm like a cat, exactly like a cat—I don't like to leave a place that I am used to, and it would have been difficult for her to manage."

"Yes, very."

"I had often been thinking, when I supposed I had to go, that she would never remember to see that the table-linen was all used in its proper turn, and to have the winter curtains changed for white ones before the sun faded them."

"You're such a comfortable, dear thing to live with," observed Valentine, now the narrative was over. "Everybody likes you, you know."

Mrs. Henfrey smiled complacently, accepting the compliment. She was, to all strangers, an absolutely uninteresting woman; but her family knew her merits, and Giles and Valentine were both particularly alive to them.

"And so here I am," continued 'sister,' "but it is a pity for poor Emily, for she wanted me to live in that house, you know, John, with her."

"But I thought old Walker was devoted to her," said John.

"So he was, my dear, so long as her boy was with her; but now she is nobody, and I am told he shows a willingness to let her go, which is almost like dismissing her."

"I hope she will not get my old woman away to live with her," thought John, with a sudden start. "I don't know what I may be driven to, if she does. I shall have to turn out of my own house, or take the Golden Head into it by way of protection. No, not that! I'll play the man. But," he thought, continuing his cogitations, "Emily is too young and attractive to live alone, and what so natural as that she should ask her old aunt to come to her?"

John was still deeply cogitating on this knotty point when the children came back, and conducted him and Valentine to the place where Brandon was at work, and Dorothea sitting near him on a tree-stump knitting.

None of the party ever forgot that afternoon, but each remembered it as an appeal to his own particular circumstances. Brandon was deep in the contentment of a great wish fulfilled. The newly-perfected life was fresh and sweet, and something of reserve in the character and manners of his wife seemed to restrain him from using up the charm of it too fast. His restless and passionate nature was at once satisfied and kept in check by the freshness and moderation of hers. She received his devotion very quietly, made no demonstrations, but grew to him, laid up his confidences in her heart, and let him discover—though she never said it—that all the rest of the world was becoming as nothing for his sake. Accordingly it did not occur to him, excepting on Valentine's own account, to consider how he might feel during this interview. He noticed that he was a little sulky and perhaps rather out of countenance; he did not wonder at these things; but being absolutely secure of his wife's love, he never even said to himself how impossible it was that her affection should revert to Valentine; but this was for the simple reason that he had never thought about that matter at all. He talked to Valentine on indifferent subjects, and felt that he should be glad when he had got over the awkwardness he was then evidently enduring, for they had been accustomed, far more than most brothers, to live together on terms of familiar intimacy, and only one of them at present was aware that this could never be again.

Valentine also never forgot, but often saw that picture again with the fresh fulness of the leaves for a background to the girlish figure; and the fair face so innocent and candid and so obviously content. She was seated opposite to him, with Brandon on the grass close to her. In general they addressed each other merely by the Christian name, but just before John rose to take leave, Dorothea dropped her ball. It rolled a little way, and pointing it out to Brandon with her long wooden knitting-pin, she said, in a soft quiet tone, "Love, will you pick it up?" and Valentine, who had overheard the little speech, was inexpressibly hurt, almost indignant. He could not possibly have told why, but he hoped she did not say that often, and when Brandon gave it into her hand again, and said something to her that Valentine could not hear, he felt almost as if he had been unkindly used, as if his feelings had been insulted, and he vowed that it should be a long time before he came to see them again.

"It won't do," he thought to himself. "I see this means a great deal more than I ever thought it did. I thought Giles would be jealous, and I should have to set things in a light that would satisfy him; but it is I who am jealous, and he does not care what I feel at all. She is all I could wish; but I don't know whether looking at her is most bitter or most sweet."

As for John, he had walked down to the wood as usual, in full possession of his present self, and as he supposed of his future intentions, and yet, sitting opposite to these married lovers for a quarter of an hour, wrought a certain change in him that nothing ever effaced. It was an alien feeling to him to be overcome by a yearning discontent. Something never yet fed and satisfied made its presence known to him. It was not that sense which comes to all, sooner or later, that human life cannot give us what we expected of it, but rather a passionate waking to the certainty that he never even for one day had possessed what it might have given. He had never been endowed for one day with any deep love, with its keen perceptions and high companionship.

"Well, I suppose I didn't deserve it," he thought, half angrily, while he tried to trample the feeling down and stifle it. But his keener instincts soon rose up in him and let him know that he did deserve it. It was very extraordinary that he had not won it—there were few men, indeed, who deserved it half so well.

"But it's too late now," he chose to say to himself, as he drove home. "It's not in my line either to go philandering after any woman. Besides, I hate red hair. The next *Dissolution* I'll stand for the borough of Wigfield. Seven children to bring up, and one of them almost as big as myself—what a fool I am! What can I have been thinking of?"

"What are you laughing at, papa?" said Barbara, who was sitting beside him.

"Not at you, my darling," he replied; "for you are something real."

For the next few weeks neither he nor Valentine saw much of Dorothea: excepting at three or four dinners, they scarcely met at all. After this came the Harrow holidays. Johnny came home, and with him the inevitable Crayshaw. The latter was only to stay a week, and that week should have been spent with Brandon, but the boys had begged hard to be together, having developed a peculiar friendship for one another which seemed to have been founded on many fights, in consequence of which they had been strictly forbidden to meet.

This had taken place more than a year before, when Crayshaw, having been invited by John to spend the holidays with his boy, the two had quarrelled, and even fought, to such a degree that John at last in despair had taken Johnnie over to his grandfather's house, with the declaration that if he so much as spoke to Crayshaw again, or crossed the wide brook that ran between the two houses, he would fine him half-a-crown every time he did it.

"Ith all that hateful map," said young hopeful sulkily, when he was borne off to his banishment.

"You ought to be ashamed of yourself," quoth his father. "I don't care what it's about. You have no notion of hospitality. I won't have you fight with your guest."

Crayshaw was in very weak health, but full of mischief and fun. For a few days he seemed happy enough, then he flagged, and on the fifth morning he laid half-a-crown beside John's plate at breakfast.

"What's this for?" asked John.

"Because it is not fair that he should be fined, and not I."

"Put it in the missionary box," said John, who knew very well that the boys had been constructing a dam together all the previous day.

"It was about their possessions that they quarrelled," said Gladys in giving an account of the matter afterwards. "They made a plan that they would go into partnership, and conquer all the rest of the world; but when they looked at the great map up in Parliament, and Johnnie found how much the most he had got, he said Cray must annex Japan, or he would not join. Cray said it was against his principles. So they quarrelled, and fought once or twice; but perhaps it was just as well, for you know the rest of the world would rather not be conquered. Then, when they were fined for playing together, they did every day. They made a splendid dam over the brook, which was very low; but one night came a storm, father's meadows were flooded, they could not get the dam undone, and some sheep were drowned. So they went to Grand, and begged him to tell father, and get them off. They said it was a strange thing they were never to be together, and neither of them had got a penny left. So Grand got them forgiven, and we went all over the meadows for two or three days in canoes and punts."

And now these two desirable inmates were to be together for a week. A great deal can be done in a week, particularly by those who give their minds to it because they know their time is short. That process called turning the house out of windows took place when John was away. Aunt Christie, who did not like boys, kept her distance, but Miss Crampton being very much scandalized by the unusual noise, declared, on the second morning of these holidays, that she should go up into Parliament, and see what they were all about. Miss Crampton was not supposed ever to go up into Parliament; it was a privileged place.

"Will the old girl really come, do you think?" exclaimed Crayshaw.

"She says she shall, as soon as she has done giving Janie her music lesson," replied Barbara, who had rushed up the steep stairs to give this message.

"Mon peruke!" exclaimed Johnnie looking round, "you'd better look out, then, or vous l'attraperais."

The walls were hung with pictures, maps, and caricatures; these last were what had attracted Johnnie's eyes, and the girls began hastily to cover them.

"It's very unkind of her," exclaimed Barbara. "Father never exactly said that we were to have our own playroom to ourselves, but we know, and she knows, that he meant it."

Then, after a good deal of whispering, giggling, and consulting among the elder ones, the little boys were dismissed; and in the meantime Mr. Nicholas Swan, who, standing on a ladder outside, was nailing the vines (quite aware that the governess was going to have a reception which might be called a warning never to come there any more), may or may not have intended to make his work last as long as possible. At any rate, he could with difficulty forbear from an occasional grin, while, with his nails neatly arranged between his lips, he leisurely trained and pruned; and when he was asked by the young people to bring them up some shavings and a piece of wood, he went down to help in the mischief, whatever it might be, with an alacrity ill suited to his years and gravity.

"Now, I'll tell you what, young gentlemen," he remarked, when, ascending, he showed his honest face again, thrust in a log of wood, and exhibited an armful of shavings, "I'm agreeable to anything but gunpowder, or that there spark as comes cantering out o' your engine with a crack. No, Miss Gladys, ex-cuse me, I don't give up these here shavings till I know it's all right."

"Well, well, it *ith* all right," exclaimed Johnnie, "we're not going to do any harm! O Cray, he'th brought up a log ath big ath a fiddle. Quelle alouette!"

"How lucky it is that she has never seen Cray!" exclaimed Barbara. "Johnnie, do be calm; how are we to do it, if you laugh so? Now then, you are to be attending to the electrifying machine."

"Swanny," asked Crayshaw, "have you got a pipe in your pocket? I want one to lie on my desk."

"Well, now, to think o' your asking me such a

question, just as if I was ever *known* to take so much as a whiff in working hours—no, not in the tool-house, nor nowhere."

"But just feel. Come, you might."

"Well, now, this here is remarkable," exclaimed Swan, with a start as if of great surprise, when, after feeling in several pockets, a pipe appeared from the last one.

"Don't knock the ashes out."

"She's coming," said Swan, furtively glancing down, and then pretending to nail with great diligence. "And, my word, if here isn't Miss Christie with her!"

A great scuffle now ensued to get things ready. Barbara darted down-stairs, and what she may have said to Aunt Christie while Swan received some final instructions above, is of less consequence than what Miss Crampton may have felt when she found herself at the top of the stairs in the long room, with its brown high-pitched roof—a room full of the strangest furniture, warm with the sun of August, and sweet with the scent of the creepers.

Gladys and Johnnie were busy at the electrifying machine, and with a rustling and crackling noise the "spunky little flashes," as Swan called them, kept leaping from one leaden knob to another.

Miss Crampton saw a youth sitting on a low chair, with his legs on rather a higher one; the floor under him was strewed with shavings, which looked, Swan thought, "as natural as life," meaning that they looked just as if he had made them by his own proper whittling.

The youth in question was using a large pruning knife on a log that he held rather awkwardly on his knee. He had a soft hat, which had been disposed over one eye. Miss Crampton gave the sparks as wide a berth as she could, and as she advanced, " Well, sir," Swan was saying in obedience to his instructions, " if you've been brought up a republican, I spose you can't help it. But whatever *your* notions may be, Old Master is staunch. He's all for Church and Queen, and he hates republican institootions like poison. Which is likewise my own feelings to a T."

No one had taken any notice of Miss Crampton, and she stopped amazed.

" Wall," answered the youth, diligently whittling, " I think small potatoes of ye-our lo-cation myself - but ye-our monarchical government, I guess, hez not yet corrupted the he-eart of the Grand. He handed onto me and onto his hair a tip which"—here he put his hand in his waistcoat pocket, and fondly regarded two or three coins; then feigning to become aware of Miss Crampton's presence, "Augustus John, my. yound friend," he continued, " ef yeow feel like it, I guess yeou'd better set a chair for the school marm—for it is the school marm, I calculate?"

Here Miss Christie, radiant with joy and malice, could not conceal her delight, but patted him on the shoulder, and then hastily retreated into the background, lest she should spoil the sport; while as Johnnie, having small command of countenance, did not dare to turn from the window out of which he was pretending to look, Crayshaw rose himself, shook hands with Miss Crampton, and setting a chair for her, began to whittle again.

"Wall," he then said, "and heow do yeou git along with ye-our teaching, marm? Squire thinks a heap of ye-our teaching, as I he-ear, specially ye-our teaching of the eye-talian tongue."

"Did I understand you to be arguing with the gardener when I came in, respecting the principles and opinions of this family?" inquired Miss Crampton, who had now somewhat recovered from her surprise, and was equal to the resenting of indignities.

"Wall, mebby I was, but it's a matter of science that we're mainly concerned with, I guess, this morning—science, electricity. We're gitting on first-rate —those rods on the stairs——"

"Yes?" exclaimed Miss Crampton.

"We air of a scientific turn, we air—Augustus John and I—fixing wires to every one of them. They air steep, those steps," he continued pensively.

Here Miss Crampton's colour increased visibly.

"And when the machine is che-arged, we shall electrify them. So that when yeou dew but touch one rod, it'll make yeou jump as high as the next step, without any voluntary effort. Yeou'll find that an improvement."

Here Swan ducked down, and laughed below at his ease.

"We air very scientific in my country."

"Indeed!"

"Ever been to Amurica?"

"Certainly not," answered Miss Crampton with vigour, "nor have I the slightest intention of ever doing so. Pray, are you allowed, in consideration of your nationality, to whittle in Harrow School?"

This was said by way of a reproof for the state of the floor.

"Wall," began Crayshaw, to cover the almost audible titters of the girls; but, distracted by this from the matter in hand, he coughed, went on whittling, and held his peace.

"I have often told Johnnie," said Miss Crampton with great dignity, at the same time darting a severe glance at Johnnie's back, "that the delight he takes in talking the Devonshire dialect is likely to be very injurious to his English, and he will have it that this country accent is not permanently catching. It may be hoped," she continued, looking round, "that other accents are not catching either."

Crayshaw, choosing to take this hint as a compliment, smiled sweetly. "I guess I'm speaking better than usual," he observed, "for my brother and his folks air newly come from the Ste-ates, and I've been with them. But," he continued, a sudden gleam of joy lighting up his eyes as something occurred to him that he thought suitable to "top up" with, "all the Mortimers talk with such a peowerful English ac-*cent*, that when I come de-own to this *lo*-cation, my own seems to melt off my tongue. Neow, yeou'll skasely believe it," he continued, "but it's tre-ue that ef yeou were tew hea-ar me talk at the end of a week, yeou'd he-ardly realise that I was an Amurican at all."

"Cray, how can ye?" exclaimed Aunt Christie, "and so wan as ye look this morning too."

"Seen my brother?" inquired Crayshaw meekly.

"No, I have not," said Miss Crampton bridling.

"He's merried. We settle airly in my country; it's one of our institootions." Another gleam of joy and impudence shot across the pallid face. "I'm thinking of settling shortly myself."

Then, as Aunt Christie was observed to be struggling with a laugh that, however long repressed, was sure to break forth at last, Barbara led her to the top of the stairs, and loudly entreated her to mind she didn't stumble, and to mind she did not touch the stair-rods, for the machine, she observed, was just ready.

"The jarth are all charged now, Cray," said Johnnie, coming forward at last. "Mith Crampton, would you like to have the firtht turn of going down with them?"

"No, thank you," said Miss Crampton almost suavely, and rising with something very like alacrity. Then, remembering that she had not even mentioned what she came for, "I wish to observe," she said, "that I much disapprove of the noise I hear up in Parliament. I desire that it may not occur again. If it does, I shall detain the girls in the schoolroom. I am very much disturbed by it."

"You don't say so!" exclaimed Crayshaw with an air of indolent surprise; and Miss Crampton thereupon retreated down-stairs, taking great care not to touch any metallic substance.

## CHAPTER VI.

MR. MORTIMER GOES THROUGH THE TURNPIKE.

"I hear thee speak of the happy land."

SWAN looked down as Miss Crampton and Miss Christie emerged into the garden.

"Most impertinent of Swan," he heard the former say, "to be arguing thus about political affairs in the presence of the children. And what Mr. Mortimer can be thinking of, inviting young Crayshaw to stay so much with them, I cannot imagine. We shall be having them turn republican next."

"Turn republican!" repeated Miss Christie with infinite scorn; "there's about as much chance of that as of his ever seeing his native country again, poor laddie; which is just no chance at all."

Crayshaw at this moment inquired of Swan, who had mounted his ladder step by step as Miss Crampton went on, "Is the old girl gone in? And what was she talking of?"

"Well, sir, something about republican institootions."

"Ah! and so you hate them like poison?"

"Yes, in a manner of speaking I do. But I've been a-thinking," continued Swan, taking the nails out of his lips and leaning in at the window, "I've been a-thinking as it ain't noways fair, if all men is ekal—which you're allers upholding—that you should say Swan, and I should say Mister Crayshaw."

"No, it isn't," exclaimed Crayshaw, laughing; "let's have it the other way. You shall say Crayshaw to me, and I'll say Mr. Swan to you, sir."

"Well, now, you allers contrive to get the better of me, you and Mr. Johnnie, you're so sharp! But, anyhow, I could earn my own living before I was your age, and neither of you can. Then, there's hardly a year as I don't gain a prize."

"I'm like a good clock," said Crayshaw, "I neither gain nor lose. I can strike too. But how did you find out, sir, that I never gained any prizes?"

"Don't you, sir?"

"Never, sir—I never gained one in my life, sir. But I say, I wish you'd take these shavings down again."

"No, I won't," answered Swan, "if I'm to be 'sirred' any more, and the young ladies made to laugh at me."

"Let Swanny alone, Cray," said Gladys. "Be as conservative as you like, Swan. Why shouldn't you? It's the only right thing."

"Nothing can be very far wrong as Old Master thinks," answered Swan. "He never interfered with my ways of doing my work either, no more than Mr. John does, and that's a thing I vally: and he never but once wanted me to do what I grudged doing."

"When was that?" asked Mr. Augustus John.

"Why, when he made me give up that there burial club," answered Swan. "He said it was noways a moral instootion; and so I shouldn't have even a decent burying to look forward to for me and my wife (my poor daughters being widows, and a great expense to me), if he hadn't said he'd bury us himself if I'd give it up, and bury us respectably too, it stands to reason. Mr. John heard him."

"Then, thath the thame thing ath if he'd thaid it himthelf," observed Johnnie, answering the old man's thought about a much older man.

"Did I say it wasn't, sir? No, if ever there was

a gentleman—it's not a bit of use argufying that all men are ekal. I'm not ekal to either of them two."

"In what respect?" asked Crayshaw.

"In what respect? Well, sir, this is how it is. I wouldn't do anything mean nor dishonest; but as for them two, they couldn't. I never had the education neither to be a gentleman, nor wished to. Not that I talk as these here folks do down here—I'd scorn it. I'm a Sunbury man myself, and come from the valley of the Thames, and talk plain English. But one of my boys, Joey," continued Swan, "talking of wishes, he wished he'd had better teaching. He's been very uppish for some time (all his own fault he hadn't been more edicated); told his mother and me, afore he sailed for the West Indies, as he'd been trying hard for some time to turn gentleman. 'I shall give myself all the airs that ever I can,' he says, 'when once I get out there.' 'Why, you young ass!' says I, 'for it's agen my religion to call you a fool (let alone your mother wouldn't like it), arn't you awear that giving himself airs is exactly what no real gentleman ever does?' 'A good lot of things,' says he, 'father, goes to the making of a gentleman.' 'Ay, Joey,' says I, 'but ain't a gentleman a man with good manners?

Now a good-manner'd man is allers saying by his ways and looks to them that air beneath him, "You're as good as I am!" and a bad-manner'd man is allers saying by his ways and looks to them that air above him, "I'm as good as you air!" There's a good many folks,' I says (not knowing I should repeat it to you this day, Mr. Crayshaw), 'as will have it, that because we shall all ekally have to be judged in the next world, we must be all ekal in this. In some things I uphold we air, and in others I say we're not. Now your real gentleman thinks most of them things that make men ekal, and t'other chap thinks most of what makes them unekal.'"

"Hear, hear!" said Johnnie. "And what did Joey thay to that, Thwan?"

"He didn't say much," answered Swan in his most pragmatical manner. "He knows well enough that when I'm argufying with my own children (as I've had the expense of bringing up), I expect to have the last word, and I have it. It's dinner-time, Mr. Johnnie; will you pass me out my pipe? I don't say but what I may take a whiff while the dinner's dishing up."

"It was very useful, Swan," said Gladys. "No doubt it made Miss Crampton think that Cray smokes."

"My word!" exclaimed Swan, "it was as good as a play to see him give himself those meek airs, and look so respectful."

He went down, and the two little boys came up. They had been turned out of Parliament, and had spent the time of their exile in running to the town, and laying out some of their money in the purchase of a present for Crayshaw; they were subject to humble fits of enthusiasm for Crayshaw and Johnnie. They came in, and handed him a "Robinson Crusoe" with pictures in it.

Crayshaw accepted it graciously.

"You must write my name in it," he observed, with exceeding mildness, "and mind you write it with a soft G."

"Yes, of course," said little Hugh, taking in, but hesitating how to obey.

"A hard G is quite wrong, and very indigestible too," he continued, yet more mildly; "though people will persist that it's a capital letter."

The young people then began to congratulate themselves on their success as regarded Miss Crampton.

"She scarcely stayed five minutes, and she was so afraid of the machine, and so shocked at the whittling and the talk, and Cray's whole appearance, that she will not come near us while he is here. After that, the stair-rods will protect us."

"No," said Crayshaw, "but it's no stimulus to my genius to have to talk Yankee to such ignorant people. I might mix up North, South, and West as I liked, and you would be none the wiser. However, if she chances to hear me speak a week hence, she'll believe that my accent has entirely peeled off. I thought I'd better provide against that probability. It was an invention worthy of a poet, which I am."

"Que les poètes thoient pendus," said Augustus John, with vigour and sincerity. "Ekthepting Homer and Tennython," he added, as if willing to be just to all men.

"What for? they've done nothing to you."

"Haven't they! But for them I need not watht my life in making Latin vertheth. The fighting, though, in Homer and Tennython I like."

In the meantime the four younger children were whispering together over a large paper parcel, that crackled a good deal.

"Which do you think is the grandest word?" said Bertram.

"I like *fallacious*, Janie."

"But you said you would put *umbrageous*," observed Hugh, in a discontented tone.

"No, those words don't mean *it*," answered Janie. "I like *ambrosial* best. Put ' For our dear ambrosial Johnnie.'"

The parcel contained as many squibs and crackers as the seller thereof would trust with his young customers; also one rocket.

Johnnie's little brothers and sisters having written these words, rose from the floor on which they had been seated, and with blushes and modest pride presented the parcel.

"For a birthday present," they said, "and, Johnnie, you're to let off every one of them your own self; and lots more are coming from the shop."

"My wig!" exclaimed Johnnie, feigning intense surprise, though he had heard every word of the conference. "Let them all off mythelf, did you thay? Well, I do call that a motht egregiouth and tender lark."

These epithets appeared to give rarity and splendour to his thanks. Janie pondered over them a little, but when Crayshaw added, "Quite parenthetical," she gave it up. That was a word she could not hope to understand. When a difficulty is once confessed to be unconquerable, the mind can repose before it as before difficulties overcome, so says Whately. "If it had only been as hard a word as *chemical*," thought Janie, "I would have looked it out in the spelling-book; but this word is so very hard that perhaps nobody knows it but Cray."

For the remainder of the week, though many revolutionary speeches were made in Parliament against the constituted schoolroom authorities, there was, on the whole, better behaviour and less noise.

After that, John took his three elder children on the Continent, keeping the boy with him till Harrow School opened again, and remaining behind with the girls till the first week in November. During this time he by no means troubled himself about the domestic happiness that he felt he had missed, though he looked forward with fresh interest to the time when his intelligent little daughters would be companions for him, and began, half unconsciously, to idealise the character of his late wife, as if her death had cost him a true companion—as if, in fact, it had not made him much nobler and far happier.

He was not sorry, when he returned home, to find Valentine eager to get away for a little while, for it had been agreed that the old man should not be left by both of them. Valentine was improved; his comfortable and independent position in his uncle's house, where his presence was so evidently regarded as an advantage, had made him more satisfied with himself; and absence from Dorothea had enabled him to take an interest in other women.

He went away in high spirits and capital health, and John subsided into his usual habits, his children continuing to grow about him. He was still a head taller than his eldest son, but this did not promise to be long the case. And his eldest girls were so clever, and so forward with their education, that he was increasingly anxious to propitiate Miss Crampton. It was very difficult to hold the balance even; he scarcely knew how to keep her at a distance, and yet to mark his sense of her value.

"I am going to see the Brandons to-morrow," he remarked to Miss Christie one day, just before the Christmas holidays.

"Then I wish ye would take little Nancy with ye," observed the good lady, "for Dorothea was here yesterday: Emily is come to stay with them, and she drove her over. Emily wished to see the child, and when she found her gone out for her walk she was disappointed."

"What did she want with her?" asked John.

"Well, I should have thought it might occur to ye that the sweet lamb had perhaps some sacred reason for feeling attracted towards the smallest creatures she could conveniently get at."

"Let the nestling bird be dressed up, then," said John. "I will drive her over with me to lunch this morning. Poor Emily! she will feel seeing the child."

"Not at all. She has been here twice to see the two little ones. At first she would only watch them over the blinds, and drop a few tears; but soon she felt the comfort of them, and when she had got a kiss or two, she went away more contented."

Accordingly John drove his smallest daughter over to Wigfield House, setting her down rosy and smiling from her wraps, and sending her to the ladies, while he went up to Brandon's peculiar domain to talk over some business with him.

They went down into the morning-room together,

and Emily rose to meet John. It was the first time he had seen her in her mourning-dress and with the cap that did not seem at all to belong to her.

Emily was a graceful young woman. Her face, of a fine oval shape, was devoid of ruddy hues; yet it was more white than pale; the clear dark grey eyes shining with health, and the mouth being red and beautiful. The hair was dark, abundant, and devoid of gloss, and she had the advantage of a graceful and cordial manner, and a very charming smile.

There were tears on her eyelashes when she spoke to John, and he knew that his little cherub of a child must have caused them. She presently went back to her place, taking little Anastasia on her knee; while Dorothea, sitting on the sofa close to them, and facing the child, occupied and pleased herself with the little creature, and encouraged her to talk.

Of English children this was a lovely specimen, and surely there are none lovelier in the world. Dorothea listened to her pretty tongue, and mused over her with a silent rapture. Her hair fell about her face like flakes of floss-silk, loose, and yellow as Indian corn; and her rosy cheeks were deeply dimpled. She was the only one of the Mortimers who was small for her years. She liked being nursed and petted, and while Dorothea smoothed out the fingers of her tiny gloves, the little fat hands, so soft and warm, occupied themselves with the contents of her workbox.

She was relating how Grand had invited them all to spend the day. " Papa brought the message, and they all wanted to go ; and so—" she was saying, when John caught the sound of her little voice— "and so papa said, 'What! not one of you going to stay with your poor old father?'"—these words, evidently authentic, she repeated with the deepest pathos—" and so," she went on, "I said, 'I will.'" Then, after a pause for reflection, " That was kind of me, wasn't it?"

A few caresses followed.

Then catching sight of Emily's brooch, in which was a portrait of her child, little Nancy put the wide tulle cap-strings aside, and looked at it earnestly.

"I know who that is," she said, after bestowing a kiss on the baby's face.

"Do you, my sweet? who is it, then?"

"It's Freddy ; he's gone to the happy land. It's

full of little boys and girls. Grand's going soon," she added, with great cheerfulness. "Did you know? Grand says he hopes he shall go soon."

"How did Emily look?" asked Miss Christie, when John came home.

"Better than usual, I think," said John carelessly. "There's no bitterness in her sorrow, poor thing! She laughed several times at Nancy's childish talk."

"She looks a great deal too young and attractive to live alone," said Miss Christie pointedly.

"Well," answered John, "she need not do that long. There are several fellows about here, who, unless they are greater fools than I take them for, will find her, as a well-endowed young widow, quite as attractive as they did when she was an almost portionless girl."

"But in the meantime?" said Miss Christie.

"If you are going to say anything that I shall hate to hear," answered John, half-laughing, "don't keep me lingering long. If you mean to leave me, say so at once, and put me out of my misery."

"Well, well," said Miss Christie, looking at him with some pleasure, and more admiration, "I've been torn in pieces for several weeks past, thinking it over.

Never shall I have my own way again in any man's house, or woman's either, as I have had it here. And the use of the carriage and the top of the pew," she continued, speaking to herself as much as to him; "and the keys; and I always *knew* I was welcome, which is more than being told so. And I thank ye, John Mortimer, for it all, I do indeed; but if my niece's daughter is wanting me, what can I do but go to her?"

"It was very base of Emily not to say a word about it," said John, smiling with as much grimness as utter want of practice, together with the natural cast of his countenance, would admit of.

Miss Christie looked up, and saw with secret joy the face she admired above all others coloured with a sudden flush of most unfeigned vexation. John gave the footstool before him a little shove of impatience, and it rolled over quite unknown to him, and lighted on Miss Christie's corns.

She scarcely felt the pain. It was sweet to be of so much importance. Two people contending for one lonely, homely old woman.

"Say the word," she presently said, "and I won't leave ye."

"No," answered John, "you ought to go to Emily. I had better say instead that I am very sensible of the kindness you have done me in staying so long."

"But ye won't be driven to do anything rash?" she answered, observing that he was still a little chafed, and willing to pass the matter off lightly.

"Such as taking to myself the lady up-stairs!" exclaimed John. "No, but I must part with her; if one of you goes, the other must."

This was absolutely the first time the matter had even been hinted at between them, and yet Miss Christie's whole conduct was arranged with reference to it, and John always fully counted on her protective presence.

"Ay, but if I might give myself the liberty of a very old friend," she answered, straightway taking the ell because he had given her an inch, "there is something I would like to say to ye."

"What would you like to say?"

"Well, I would like to say that if a man is so more than commonly a fine man, that it's just a pleasure to set one's eyes on him, and if he's well endowed with this world's gear, it's a strange thing if there is no excellent, desirable, and altogether sweet young woman ready, and even sighing, for him."

"Humph!" said John.

"I don't say there is," proceeded Miss Christie; "far be it from me."

"I hate red hair," answered the attractive widower.

"It's just like a golden oriole. It isn't red at all," replied Miss Christie dogmatically.

"*I* call it red," said John Mortimer.

"The painters consider it the finest colour possible," continued the absent lady's champion.

"Then let them paint her," said John; "but—I shall not marry her; besides," he chose to say, "I know if I asked her she would not have me: therefore, as I don't mean to ask her, I shall not be such an unmannerly dog as to discuss her, further than to say that I do not wish to marry a woman who takes such a deep and sincere interest in herself."

"Why, don't we all do that? I am sure *I* do."

"You naturally feel that you are the most important and interesting of all God's creatures *to yourself*. You do not therefore think that you must be so to *me*. Our little lives, my dear lady, should not turn round upon themselves, and as it were make a centre of their own axis. The better lives revolve round some external centre; everything depends on that centre, and how much or how many we carry round with us besides ourselves. Now, my father's centre is and always has been Almighty God—our Father and his. His soul is as it were drawn to God and lost, as a centre to itself in that great central soul. He looks at everything—I speak it reverently—from God's high point of view."

"Ay, but she's a good woman," said Miss Christie, trying to adopt his religious tone, and as usual not knowing how. "Always going about among the poor. I don't suppose," she continued with enthusiasm—"I don't suppose there's a single thing they can do in their houses that she doesn't interfere with." Then observing his amusement, "Ye don't know what's good for ye," she added, half laughing, but a little afraid she was going too far.

"If ever I am so driven wild by the governesses that I put my neck, as a heart-broken father, under the yoke, in order to get somebody into the house who can govern as you have done," said John, "it will be entirely your doing, your fault for leaving me."

"Well, well," said Miss Christie, laughing, "I must abide ye're present reproaches, but I feel that I need dread no future ones, for if ye should go and do it, ye'll be too much a gentleman to say anything to me afterwards."

"You are quite mistaken," exclaimed John, laughing, "that one consolation I propose to reserve to myself, or if I should not think it right to speak, mark my words, the more cheerful I look the more sure you may be that I am a miserable man."

Some days after this the stately Miss Crampton departed for her Christmas holidays, a letter following her, containing a dismissal (worded with studied politeness) and a cheque for such an amount of money as went far to console her.

"Mr. Mortimer was about to send the little boys to school, and meant also to make other changes in his household. Mr. Mortimer need hardly add, that should Miss Crampton think of taking another situation, he should do himself the pleasure to speak as highly of her qualifications as she could desire."

Aunt Christie gone, Miss Crampton gone also! What a happy state of things for the young Mortimers. If Crayshaw had been with them, there is no saying what they might have done; but Johnnie, by his father's orders, had brought a youth of seventeen to spend three weeks with him, and the young fellow turned out to be such a dandy, and so much better pleased to be with the girls than with Johnnie scouring the country and skating, that John for the first time began to perceive the coming on of a fresh source of trouble in his house. Gladys and Barbara were nearly fourteen years old, but looked older; they were tall, slender girls, black-haired and grey-eyed, as their mother had been, very simple, full of energy, and in mind and disposition their father's own daughters. Johnnie groaned over his unpromising companion, Edward Conyngham by name; but he was the son of an old friend, and John did what he could to make the boys companionable, while the girls, though they laughed at young Conyngham, were on the whole more amused with his compliments than their father liked. But it was not till one day, going up into Parliament, and finding some verses pinned on a curtain, that he began to feel what it was to have no lady to superintend his daughters.

"What are they?" Gladys said. "Why, papa,

Cray sent them; they are supposed to have been written by Conyngham."

"What does he know about Conyngham?"

"Oh, I told him when I last wrote."

"When you last wrote," repeated John, in a cogitative tone.

"Yes; I write about once a fortnight, of course, when Barbara writes to Johnnie."

"Did Miss Crampton superintend the letters?" was John's next inquiry.

"Oh no, father, we always wrote them up here."

"I wonder whether Janie would have allowed this," thought John. "I suppose as they are so young it cannot signify."

"Cray sent them because we told him how Conyngham walked after Gladys wherever she went. That boy is such a goose, father; you never heard such stuff as he talks when you are away."

John was silent.

"Johnnie and Cray are disgusted with his rubbish," continued Barbara, "pretending to make love and all that."

"Yes," said John; "it is very ridiculous. Boys like Conyngham and Crayshaw ought to know better."

Nothing, he felt, could be so likely to make the schoolroom distasteful to his daughters as this early admiration. Still he was consoled by the view they took of it.

"Cray does know better, of course," said Gladys carelessly.

"Still, he was extremely angry with Conyngham, for being so fond of Gladys," remarked Barbara; "because you know she is *his* friend. He would never hear about his puppy, that old Patience Smith takes care of for sixpence a week, or his rabbits that we have here, or his hawk that lives at Wigfield, unless Gladys wrote; Mr. Brandon never writes to him."

"Now shall I put a stop to this, or shall I let it be?" thought John; and he proceeded to read Crayshaw's effusion.

### TO G. M. IN HER BRONZE BOOTS.

As in the novel skippers say,
"Shiver my timbers!" and "Belay!"
While a few dukes so handy there
Respectfully make love or swear;

As in the poem some great ass
For ever pipes to his dear lass;
And as in life tea crowns the cup,
And muffins sop much butter up;

So, naturally, while I walk
With you, I feel a swell—and stalk—
Consecutively muttering "Oh,
I'm quite a man, I feel I grow."

> But loudliest thumps this heart to-day,
> While in the mud you pick your way,
> (You fawn, you flower, you star, you gem,)
> In your new boots with heels to them.
>      Your Eldest Slave.

"I don't consider these verses a bit more *consecutive* than Conyngham's talk," said John, laughing.

"Well, father, then he shouldn't say such things! He said Mr. Brandon walked with an infallible stride, and that you were the most consecutive of any one he had ever met with."

"But, my dear little girl, Crayshaw would not have known that unless you had told him; do you think that was the right thing to do by a guest?"

Gladys blushed. "But, father," said Barbara, "I suppose Cray may come now; Conyngham goes to-morrow. Cray never feels so well as when he is here."

"I had no intention of inviting him this Christmas," answered John.

"Well," said Gladys, "it doesn't make much difference; he and Johnnie can be together just the same nearly all day, because his brother and Mrs. Crayshaw are going to stay with the Brandons, and Cray is to come too."

John felt as if the fates were against him.

"And his brother was so horribly vexed when he found that he hardly got on at school at all."

"That's enough to vex any man. Cray should spend less time in writing these verses of his."

"Yes, he wrote us word that his brother said so, and was extremely cross and unpleasant, when he replied that this was genius, and must not be repressed."

John, after this, rode into the town, and as he stopped his horse to pay the turnpike, he was observed by the turnpike-keeper's wife to be looking gloomy and abstracted; indeed, the gate was no sooner shut behind him than he sighed, and said with a certain bitterness, "I shouldn't wonder if, in two or three years' time, I am driven to put my neck under the yoke after all."

"No, we can't come," said little Hugh, when a few days after this Emily and Dorothea drove over and invited the children to spend the day, "we couldn't come on any account, because something very grand is going to happen."

"Did you know," asked Anastasia, "that Johnnie had got into the *shell?*"

"No, my sweet," said Emily, consoling her empty

arms for their loss, and appeasing her heart with a kiss.

"And father always said that some day he should come home to early dinner," continued Hugh, "and show the great magic lantern up in Parliament. Then Swan's grandchildren and the coachman's little girls are coming; and every one is to have a present. It will be such fun."

"The shell," observed Bertram, "means a sort of a class between the other classes. Father's so glad Johnnie has got into the shell."

"She is glad too," said Anastasia. "You're glad, Mrs. Nemily."

"Yes, I am glad," answered Emily, a tear that had gathered under her dark eyelashes falling, and making her eyes look brighter, and her smile more sweet.

Emily was not of a temperament that is ever depressed. She had her times of sorrow and tears; but she could often smile, and still oftener laugh.

## CHAPTER VII.

#### THE RIVER.

"Now there was a great calm at that time in the river; wherefore Mr. Standfast, when he was about half way in, he stood awhile, and talked to his companions that had waited upon him thither; and he said, . . . 'I have formerly lived by hearsay and faith; but now I go where I shall live by sight, and shall be with Him in whose company I delight myself. I have loved to hear my Lord spoken of; and wherever I have seen the print of his shoe in the earth, there have I coveted to set my foot too.'"—*Pilgrim's Progress.*

AND now the Christmas holidays being more than half over, Mr. Augustus Mortimer desired that his grandson might come and spend a few days with him, for Valentine had told him how enchanted John was with the boy's progress, but that he was mortified almost past bearing by his lisp. Grand therefore resolved that something should be done; and Crayshaw having now arrived, and spending the greater part of every day with his allies the young Mortimers, was easily included in the invitation. If anybody wants a school-boy, he is generally most welcome to him. Grand sent a flattering message to the effect that he should be much disappointed if Cray did not appear that day at his dinner table. Cray accordingly did appear, and after dinner the old man began to put before his grandson the advantage it would be to him if he could cure himself of his lisp.

"I never lithp, Grand," answered the boy, "when I talk thlowly, and—— No, I mean when I talk s-lowly and take pains."

"Then why don't you always talk slowly and take pains, to please your father, to please me, and to improve yourself?"

Johnnie groaned.

"This is very little more than an idle childish habit," continued Grand.

"We used to think it would do him good to have his tongue slit," said Crayshaw, "but there's no need. When I torment him and chaff him, he never does it."

"I hope there *is* no need," said Grand, a little uncertain whether this remedy was proposed in joke or earnest. "Valentine has been reminding me that he used to lisp horribly when a child, but he entirely cured himself before he was your age."

Johnnie, in school-boy fashion, made a face at Valentine when the old man was not looking. It expressed good-humoured defiance and derision, but the only effect it produced was on himself, for it disturbed for the moment the great likeness to his grandfather that grew on him every day. John had clear features, thick light hair, and deep blue eyes. His son was dark, with bushy eyebrows, large stern features, and a high narrow head, like old Grand.

It was quite dark, and the depth of winter, but the thermometer was many degrees above freezing-point, and a warm south wind was blowing. Grand rose and rang the bell. "Are the stable lanterns lighted?" he asked.

"Yes, sir."

"Then you two boys come with me."

The boys, wondering and nothing loth, followed to the stable, and the brown eyes of two large ponies looked mildly into theirs.

"Trot them out," said Grand to the groom, "and let the young gentlemen have a good look at them."

Not a word did either of the boys say. An event of huge importance appeared to loom in the horizon of each: he cogitated over its probable conditions.

"I got a saddle for each of them," said Grand. "Valentine chose them, Johnnie. There now, we had better come in again." And when they were seated in the dining-room as before, and there was still silence, he went on, " You two, as I understand, are both in the same house at Harrow ?"

" Yes, sir."

" And it is agreed that Johnnie could cure himself of his lisp if he chose, and if you would continually remind him of it ?"

" Oh yes, certainly it is."

" Very well, if the thing is managed by next Easter, I'll give each of you one of those ponies ; and," continued Grand cunningly, " you may have the use of them during the remainder of these holidays, provided you both promise, upon your honour, to begin the cure directly. If Johnnie has not left off lisping at Easter, I shall have the ponies sold."

" I'll lead him such a life that he shall wish he'd never been born ; I will indeed," exclaimed Crayshaw fervently.

" Well," said Johnnie, " never wath a better time. *Allez le,* or, in other wordth, go it."

" And every two or three days you shall bring him to me," continued Grand, " that I may hear him read and speak."

The next morning, before John went into the town, he was greeted by the two boys on their ponies, and came out to admire and hear the conditions.

"We mayn't have them at school," said Johnnie, bringing out the last word with laudable distinctness, "but Grand will let them live in hith—in his—stables."

John was very well contented to let the experiment alone; and a few days after this, his younger children, going over with a message to Johnnie, reported progress to him in the evening as he sat at dinner.

"Johnnie and Cray were gone into the town on their grand new ponies, almost as big as horses; they came galloping home while we were there," said Janie.

"And, father, they are going to show up their exercises, or something that they've done, to Grand to-morrow; you'll hear them," observed Hugh.

"But poor Cray was so ill on Saturday," said the little girl, "that he couldn't do nothing but lie in bed and write his poetry."

"But they got on very well," observed Bertram philosophically. "They had up the stable-boy with a great squirt; he had to keep staring at Cray while

Johnnie read aloud, and every time Cray winked he was to squirt Johnnie. Cray didn't have any dinner or any tea, and his face was so red."

"Poor fellow!"

"Yes," said the youngest boy, "and he wrote some verses about Johnnie, and said they were for him to read aloud to grandfather. But what do you think? Johnnie said he wouldn't! That doesn't sound very kind, does it?"

Johnnie's resolution, however, was not particularly remarkable; the verses, compounded during an attack of asthma, running as follows:—

### AUGUSTUS JOHN CONFESSES TO LOSS OF APPETITE.

> I cannot eat rice pudding now,
>   Jam roll, boiled beef, and such;
> From Stilton cheese this heart I vow
>   Turns coldly as from Dutch.
>
> For crab, a shell-fish erst loved well,
>   I do not care at all,
> Though I myself am in the shell
>   And fellow-feelings call.
>
> I mourn not over tasks unsaid—
>   This child is not a flat—
> My purse is empty as my head,
>   But no—it isn't that
>
> I cannot eat. And why? To shrink
>   From truth is like a sinner,
> I'll speak or burst; it is, I think,
>   That I've just had my dinner.

Crayshaw was very zealous in the discharge of his

promise; the ponies took a great deal of exercise; and old Grand, before the boys were dismissed to school, saw very decided and satisfactory progress on the part of his grandson, while the ponies were committed to his charge with a fervour that was almost pathetic. It was hard to part from them; but men are tyrannical; they will not permit boys to have horses at a public school; the boys therefore returned to their work, and the ponies were relieved from theirs, and entered on a course of life which is commonly called eating their heads off.

John in the meanwhile tried in vain to supply the loss of the stately and erudite Miss Crampton. He wanted two ladies, and wished that neither should be young. One must be able to teach his children and keep them in order; the other must superintend the expenditure and see to the comforts of his whole household, order his children's dress, and look after their health.

Either he was not fortunate in his applicants, or he was difficult to please, for he had not suited himself with either lady when a new source of occupation and anxiety sprung up, and everything else was set aside on account of it; for all on a sudden it was perceived one afternoon that Mr. Augustus Mortimer was not at all well.

It was after bank hours, but he was dozing in his private sitting-room at the bank, and his young nephew, Mr. Mortimer, was watching him.

Valentine had caused his card to be printed "Mr. Mortimer:" he did not intend because he was landless, and but for his uncle's bounty almost penniless, to forego the little portion of dignity which belonged to him.

The carriage stood at the door, and the horses now and then stamped in the lightly-falling snow, and were sometimes driven a little way down the street and back again to warm them.

At his usual time John had gone home, and then his father, while waiting for the carriage, had dropped asleep.

Though Valentine had wakened him more than once, and told him the men and horses were waiting he had not shown any willingness to move.

"There's plenty of time; I must have this sleep out first," he said.

Then, when for the third time Valentine woke him, he roused himself. "I think I can say it now," he observed. " I could not go home, you know, Val, till it was said."

" Till what was said, uncle?"

" I forget," was the answer. " You must help me."

Valentine suggested various things which had been discussed that day; but they did not help him, and he sank into thought.

" I hope I was not going to make any mistake," he shortly said, and Valentine began to suppose he really had something particular to say. " I think my dear brother and I decided for ever to hold our peace," he next murmured, after a long pause.

Valentine was silent. The allusion to his father made him remember how completely all the more active and eventful part of their lives had gone by for these two old men before he came into the world.

' What were you and John talking of just before he left?" said the old man, after a puzzled pause.

" Nothing of the least consequence," answered Valentine, feeling that he had forgotten what he might have meant to say. " John would be uneasy if he knew you were here still. Shall we go home?"

" Not yet. If I mentioned this, you would never

tell it to my John. There is no need that my John should ever have a hint of it. You will promise not to tell him?"

"No, my dear uncle, indeed I could not think of such a thing," said Valentine, now a little uneasy. If his uncle really had something important to say, this was a strange request, and if he had not, his thoughts must be wandering.

"Well," said Grand, in a dull, quiet voice, as of one satisfied and persuaded, "perhaps it is no duty of mine, then, to mention it. But what was it that you and John were talking of just before he went away?"

"You and John were going to send your cards, to inquire after Mrs. A'Court, because she is ill. I asked if mine might go too, and as it was handed across you took notice of what was on it, and said it pleased you; do you remember? But John laughed about it."

"Yes; and what did you answer, Val?"

I said that if everybody had his rights, that ought not to have been my name at all. You ought to have been Mr. Mortimer now, and I Mr. Melcombe.

"I thought it was that," answered Grand, cogitating

"Yes, it was never intended that you should touch a shilling of that property."

"I know that, uncle," said Valentine. "My father always told me he had no expectations from his mother. It was unlucky for me, that's all. I don't mean to say," he continued, "that it has been any particular disappointment, because I was always brought up to suppose I should have nothing; but as I grow older I often think it seems rather a shame I should be cut out; and as my father was, I am sure, one of the most amiable of men, it is very odd that he never contrived to make it up with the old lady."

"He never had any quarrel with her," answered old Augustus. "He was always her favourite son."

Valentine looked at him with surprise. He appeared to be oppressed with the lassitude of sleep, and yet to be struggling to keep his eyes open and to say something. But he only managed to repeat his last words. "I've told John all that I wish him to know," he next said, and then succumbed and was asleep again.

"'The favourite son, and natural heir!" thought Valentine. "No quarrel, and yet not inherit a shilling! That is queer, to say the least of it. I'll go up to

London and have another look at that will. And he has told John something or other. Unless his thoughts are all abroad then, he must have been alluding to two perfectly different things."

" Valentine now went to the carriage and fetched in the footman, hoping that at sight of him his uncle might be persuaded to come home; but this was done with so much difficulty that, when at last it was accomplished, Valentine sent the carriage on to fetch John, and sat anxiously watching till he came, and a medical man with him.

Sleep and weakness, but no pain, and no disquietude. It was so at the end of a week; it was so at the end of a fortnight, and then it became evident that his sight was failing; he was not always aware whether or not he was alone; he often prayed aloud also, but sometimes supposed himself to be recovering.

"Where is Valentine?" he said one afternoon, when John, having left him to get some rest, Valentine had taken his place. "Are we alone?" he asked, when Valentine had spoken to him. "What time is it?"

"About four o'clock, uncle; getting dusk, and snow falls."

"Yes, I heard you mention snow when the nurse went down to her tea. I am often aware of John's presence when I cannot show it. Tell him so."

"Yes, I will."

"He is a dear good son to me."

"Yes."

"He ought not to make a sorrow of my removal. It disturbs me sometimes to perceive that he does. He knows where my will is, and all my papers. I have never concealed anything from him; I had never any cause."

"No, indeed, uncle."

"Till now," proceeded old Augustus. Valentine looked attentively in the failing light at the majestic wreck of the tall, fine old man. He made out that he eyes were closed, and that the face had its usual immobile, untroubled expression, and the last words startled him. "I have thought it best," he continued, "not to leave you anything in my will."

"No," said Valentine, "because you gave me that two thousand pounds during your lifetime."

"Yes, my dear; my memory does not fail me. John will not be cursed with one guinea of ill-gotten wealth. Valentine!"

"Yes, uncle, yes; I am here; I am not going away."

"You have the key of my cabinet, in the library. Go and fetch me a parcel that is in the drawer inside."

"Let me ring, then, first for some one to come; for you must not be left alone."

".Leave me, I say, and do as I tell you."

Valentine, vexed, but not able to decline, ran down in breathless haste, found the packet of that peculiar sort and size usually called a banker's parcel, locked the cabinet, and returned to the old man's bed.

"Are we alone?" he asked, when Valentine had made his presence known to him. "Let me feel that parcel. Ah, your father was very dear to me. I owe everything to him—everything."

Valentine, who was not easy as to what would come next, replied like an honourable man, "So you said, uncle, when you generously gave me that two thousand pounds."

"Ill-gotten wealth," old Augustus murmured, "never prospers; it is a curse to its possessor. My son, my John, will have none of it. Valentine!"

"Yes."

"What do you think was the worst-earned money that human fingers ever handled?"

The question so put suggested but one answer.

"*That* thirty pieces of silver," said Valentine.

"Ah!" replied Augustus with a sigh. "Well, thank God, none of us can match that crime. But murders have been done, and murderers have profited by the spoil! When those pieces of silver were lying on the floor of the temple, after the murderer was dead, to whom do you think they belonged?"

Valentine was excessively startled; the voice seemed higher and thinner than usual, but the conversation had begun so sensibly, and the wrinkled hand kept such firm hold still of the parcel, that it surprised him to feel, as he now did, that his dear old uncle was wandering, and he answered nothing.

"Not to the priests," continued Augustus, and as a pause followed, Valentine felt impelled to reply.

"No," he said, "they belonged to his family, no doubt, if they had chosen to pick them up."

"Ah, that is what I suppose. If his father, poor wretch, or perhaps his miserable mother, had gone into the temple that day, it would have been a strange sight, surely, to see her gather them up."

"Yes," said Valentine faintly. The shadow of something too remote to make its substance visible appeared to fall over him then, causing him a vague wonder and awe, and revulsion of feeling. He knew not whether this old man was taking leave of sober daylight reason, or whether some fresh sense of the worthlessness of earthly wealth, more especially ill-gotten wealth, had come to him from a sudden remembrance of this silver—or——

He tried gently to lead his thoughts away from what seemed to be troubling him, for his head turned restlessly on the pillow.

"You have no need to think of that," he said kindly and quietly, "for as you have just been saying, John will inherit nothing but well-earned property."

"John does not know of this," said Augustus. "I have drawn it out for years by degrees, as he supposed, for household expenses. It is all in Bank of England notes. Every month that I lived it would have become more and more."

Uncommonly circumstantial this!

"It contains seventeen hundred pounds; take it in your hand, and hear me."

"Yes, uncle."

"You cannot live on a very small income. You have evidently very little notion of the value of money. You and John may not agree. It may not suit him to have you with him; on the other hand— on the other hand—what was I saying?"

"That it might not suit John to have me with him."

"Yes, yes; but, on the other hand (where is it gone), on the other hand, it might excite his curiosity, his surprise, if I left you more in my will. Now what am I doing this for? What is it? Daniel's son? Yes."

"Dear uncle, try to collect your thoughts; there is something you want me to do with this money, try to tell me what it is."

"Have you got it in your hand?"

"Yes, I have."

"Keep it then, and use it for your own purposes."

"Thank you. Are you sure that is what you meant? Is that all?"

"Is that all? No. I said you were not to tell John."

"Will you tell him yourself then?" asked Valentine.

"I do not think he would mind my having it."

By way of answer to this, the old man actually laughed. Valentine had thought he was long past that, but it was a joyful laugh, and almost exultant.

"Mind," he said, "my John! No; you attend to my desire, and to all I have said. Also it is agreed between me and my son that if ever you two part company, he is to give you a thousand pounds. I tell you this that you may not suppose it has anything to do with the money in that parcel. Your father was everything to me," he continued, his voice getting fainter, and his speech more confused, as he went on. "and—and I never expected to see him again in this world. And so you have come over to see me, Daniel? Give me your hand. Come over to see me, and there are no lights! God has been very good to me, brother, and I begin to think He will call me into his presence soon."

Valentine started up, and it was really more in order to carry out the old man's desires, so solemnly expressed, than from any joy of possession, that he put the parcel into his pocket before he rang for the nurse and went to fetch John.

He had borne a part in the last-sustained conversation the old man ever held, and that day month, in just such a snow-storm as had fallen about his much-loved brother, his stately white head was laid in the grave.

## CHAPTER VIII.

### THE DEAD FATHER ENTREATS.

*"Prospero. I have done nothing but in care of thee,
Of thee, my dear one."*
*The Tempest.*

VALENTINE rose early the morning after the funeral; John Mortimer had left him alone in the house, and gone home to his children.

John had regarded the impending death of his father more as a loss and a misfortune than is common. He and the old man, besides being constant companions, had been very intimate friends, and the rending of the tie between them was very keenly felt by the son.

Nothing, perhaps, differs more than the amount of affection felt by different people; there is no gauge for it—language cannot convey it. Yet instinctive perception shows us where it is great. Some feel little, and show all that little becomingly; others feel much, and reveal scarcely anything; but, on the whole, men are not deceived, each gets the degree of help and sympathy that was due to him.

Valentine had been very thoughtful for John; the invitations and orders connected with a large funeral had been mainly arranged by him.

Afterwards, he had been present at the reading of the will, and had been made to feel that the seventeen hundred pounds in that parcel which he had not yet opened could signify nothing to a son who was to enter on such a rich inheritance as it set forth and specified.

Still he wished his uncle had not kept the giving of it a secret, and, while he was dressing, the details of that last conversation, the falling snow, the failing light, and the high, thin voice, changed, and yet so much more impressive for the change, recurred to his thoughts more freshly than ever, perhaps because before he went down he meant to open the parcel, which accordingly he did.

Bank of England notes were in it, and not a line of writing on the white paper that enfolded them. He turned it over, and then mechanically began to count and add up the amount. Seventeen hundred pounds, neither more nor less, and most assuredly his own. With the two thousand pounds he already possessed, this sum would, independently of any exertions of his own, bring him in nearly two hundred a-year. In case of failing health this would be enough to live on modestly, either in England or on the Continent.

He leaned his chin on his hand, and, with a dull contentment, looked at these thin, crisp papers. He had cared for his old uncle very much, and been exceedingly comfortable with him, and now that he was forbidden to mention his last gift, he began to feel (though this had fretted him at first) that it would make him more independent of John.

But why should the old father have disliked to excite his son's surprise and curiosity? Why, indeed, when he had laughed at the notion of John's being capable of minding his doing as he pleased.

Valentine pondered over this as he locked up his property. It was not yet eight o'clock, and as he put out the candle he had lighted to count his notes by (for the March morning was dark), he heard wheels, and, on going down, met John in the hall. He had come in before the breakfast-hour, as had often been his custom when he meant to breakfast with his father.

John's countenance showed a certain agitation. Valentine observing it, gave him a quiet, matter-of-fact greeting, and talked of the weather. A thaw had come on, and the snow was melting rapidly. For the moment John seemed unable to answer, but when they got into the dining-room, he said—

"I overtook St. George's groom. He had been to my house, he said, thinking you were there. Your brother sent a message, rather an urgent one, and this note to you. He wants you, it seems."

"Wants me, wants ME!" exclaimed Valentine. What for?"

John shrugged his shoulders.

"Is he ill?" continued Valentine.

"The man did not say so."

Valentine read the note. It merely repeated that his brother wanted him. What an extraordinary piece of thoughtlessness this seemed! Brandon might have perceived that Valentine would be much needed by John that day.

"You told me yesterday," said Valentine, "that there were various things you should like me to do for you in the house to-day, and over at the town too. So I shall send him word that I cannot go.'

"I think you had better go," said John.

Valentine was sure that John would have been glad of his company. It would be easier for a man with his peculiarly keen feelings not to have to face all his clerks alone the first time after his father's death.

"You must go," he repeated, however. "St. George would never have thought of sending for you unless for some urgent reason. If you take my dog-cart you will be in time for the breakfast there, which is at nine. The horse is not taken out."

Valentine still hesitating, John added—

"But, I may as well say now that my father's removal need make no difference in our being together. As far as I am concerned, I am very well pleased with our present arrangement. I find in you an aptitude for business affairs that I could by no means have anticipated. So if St. George wants to consult you about some new plan for you (which I hardly think can be the case), you had better hear what I have to say before you turn yourself out."

Valentine thanked him cordially. Emily had pointedly said to him, during his uncle's last illness, that in the event of any change, she should be pleased if he would come and live with her. He had made no answer, because he had not thought John would wish the connection between them to continue. But now everything was easy. His dear old uncle had left him a riding-horse, and some books. He had only to move these to Emily's house, and so without trouble enter another home.

It was not yet nine o'clock when Valentine entered the dining-room in his brother's house.

The gloom was over, the sun had burst forth, lumps of snow, shining in the dazzle of early sunlight, were falling with a dull thud from the trees, while every smaller particle dislodged by a waft of air, dropped with a flash as of a diamond.

First Mrs. Henfrey came in and looked surprised to see Valentine; wondered he had left John; had never seen a man so overcome at his father's funeral. Then Giles came in with some purple and some orange crocuses, which he laid upon his wife's plate. He said nothing about his note, but went and fetched Dorothea, who was also evidently surprised to see Valentine.

How lovely and interesting she looked in his eyes that morning, so serene herself, and an object of such watchful solicitude both to her husband and his old step-sister!

"Any man may feel interested in her now," thought Valentine, excusing himself to himself for the glow of admiring tenderness that filled his heart. "Sweet thing! Oh! what a fool I have been!"

There was little conversation; the ladies were in mourning, and merely asked a few questions as to the arrangements of the late relative's affairs.

Brandon sat at the head of the table, and his wife at his right hand. There was something very cordial in his manner, but such an evident turning away from any mention of having sent for him, that Valentine, perceiving the matter to be private, followed his lead, and when breakfast was over went with him up-stairs to his long room, at the top of the house, his library and workshop.

"Now, then," he exclaimed, when at last the door was shut and they were alone, "I suppose I may speak? What can it be, old fellow, that induced you to send for me at a time so peculiarly inconvenient to John?"

"It was partly something that I read in a newspaper," answered Giles, "and also—also a letter. A letter that was left in my care by your father."

"Oh! then you were to give it to me after my uncle's death, were you?"

For all answer Giles said, "There it is," and Valentine, following his eyes, saw a sealed parcel, not unlike in shape and size to the one he had already opened that morning. It was lying on a small, opened desk. "Take your time, my dear fellow," said Giles, "and read it carefully. I shall come up again soon, and tell you how it came into my possession."

Thereupon he left the room, and Valentine, very much surprised, advanced to the table.

The packet was not directed to any person, but outside it was written in Brandon's clear hand, "Read by me on the 3rd of July, 18—, and sealed up the following morning. G. B."

Valentine sat down before it, broke his brother's seal, and took out a large letter, the seal of which (his father's) had already been broken. It was addressed, in his father's handwriting, "Giles Brandon, Esq., Wigfield House."

We are never so well inclined to believe in a stroke of good fortune as when one has just been dealt to us. Valentine was almost sure he was going to read of something that would prove to be to his advantage.

His uncle had behaved so strangely in providing him with his last bounty, that it was difficult for him not to connect this letter with that gift. Something might have been made over to his father on his behalf, and, with this thought in his mind, he unfolded the sheet of foolscap and read as follows:—

"My much-loved Son,—You will see by the date of this letter that my dearest boy Valentine is between seventeen and eighteen years of age when I write it. I perceive a possible peril for him, and my brother being old, there is no one to whom I can so naturally appeal on his behalf as to you.

"I have had great anxiety about you lately, but now you are happily restored to me from the sea, and I know that I may fully trust both to your love and your discretion.

"Some men, my dear Giles, are happy enough to have nothing to hide. I am not of that number; but I bless God that I can say, if I conceal aught, it is not a work of my own doing, nor is it kept secret for my own sake.

"It is now seven weeks since I laid in the grave the body of my aged mother. She left her great-grandson,

Peter Melcombe, the only son of my nephew Peter Melcombe, whose father was my fourth brother, her sole heir.

"I do not think it wise to conceal from you that I, being her eldest surviving son, desired of her, that she would not—I mean, that I forbad my mother to leave her property to me.

"It is not for me to judge her. I have never done so, for in her case I know not what I could have done; but I write this in the full confidence that both of you will respect my wishes; and that you, Giles, will never divulge my secret, even to Valentine, unless what I fear should come to pass, and render this necessary.

"If Peter Melcombe, now a child, should live to marry, and an heir should be born to him, then throw this letter into the fire, and let it be to you as if it had never been written. If he even lives to come of age, at which time he can make a will and leave his property where he pleases, you may destroy it.

"I do not feel afraid that the child will die, it is scarcely to be supposed that he will. I pray God that it may not be so; but in case he should—in case this child should be taken away during his minority, I being already gone—then my grandfather's will is so worded that my son Valentine, my only son, will be his heir.

"Let Valentine know in such a case that I, his dead father, who delighted in him, would rather have seen him die in his cradle, than live by that land and inherit that gold. I have been poor, but I have never turned to anything at Melcombe with one thought that it could mend my case; and as I have renounced it for myself, I would fain renounce it for my heirs for ever. Nothing is so unlikely as that this property should ever fall to my son, but if it should, I trust to his love and duty to let it be, and I trust to you, Giles, to make this easy for him, either to get him away while he is yet young, to lead a fresh and manly life in some one of our colonies, or to find some career at home for him which shall provide him with a competence, that if such a temptation should come in his way, he may not find it too hard to stand against.

"And may the blessing of God light upon you for this (for I know you will do it), more than for all the other acts of dutiful affection you have ever shown me.

"When I desire you to keep this a secret (as I

hope always), I make no exception in favour of any person whatever.

"This letter is written with much thought and full deliberation, and signed by him who ever feels as a loving father towards you.

"Daniel Mortimer."

Valentine had opened the letter with a preconceived notion as to its contents, and this, together with excessive surprise, made him fail for the moment to perceive one main point that it might have told him.

When Brandon just as he finished reading came back, he found Valentine seated before the letter amazed and pale.

"What does it mean?" he exclaimed, when the two had looked searchingly at one another. "What on earth can it mean?"

"I have no idea," said Giles.

"But you have had it for years," continued Valentine, very much agitated. "Surely you have tried to find out what it means. Have you made no inquiries?"

"Yes. I have been to Melcombe. I could discover nothing at all. No," in answer to another look, "neither then, or at any other time."

"But you are older than I am, so much older, had you never any suspicion of anything at all? Did nothing ever occur before I was old enough to notice things which roused in you any suspicions?"

"Suspicions of what?"

"Of disgrace, I suppose. Of crime perhaps I mean; but I don't know what I mean. Do you think John knows of this?"

"No. I am sure he does not. But don't agitate yourself," he went on, observing that Valentine's hand trembled. "Remember, that whatever this secret was that your father kept buried in his breast, it has never been found out, that is evident, and therefore it is most unlikely now that it ever should be. In my opinion, and it is the only one I have fully formed about the matter, this crime or this disgrace—I quote your own words—must have taken place between sixty and seventy years ago, and your father expressly declares that he had nothing to do with it."

"But if the old woman had," began Valentine vehemently, and paused.

"How can that be?" answered Giles. "He says, 'I know not in her case what I could have done,' and that he has never judged her."

Valentine heaved up a mighty sigh, excitement made his pulses beat and his hands tremble.

"What made you think," he said, "that it was so long ago? I am so surprised that I cannot think coherently."

"To tell you why I think so, is to tell you something more that I believe you don't know."

"Well," said the poor fellow, sighing restlessly, "out with it, Giles."

"Your father began life by running away from home."

"Oh, I know that."

"You do?"

"Yes, my dear father told it to me some weeks before he died, but I did not like it, I wished to dismiss it from my thoughts."

"Indeed! but will you try to remember now, how he told it to you and what he said."

"It was very simple. Though now I come to think of it, with this new light thrown upon it—— Yes; he did put it very oddly, very strangely, so that I did not like the affair, or to think of it. He said that as there was now some intercourse between us and Melcombe, a place that he had not gone near for so very many years, it was almost certain, that, sooner or later,

I should hear something concerning himself that would surprise me. It was singular that I had not heard it already. I did not like to hear him talk in his usual pious way of such an occurrence; for though of course we know that all things *are* overruled for good to those who love God——"

"Well?" said Brandon, when he paused to ponder.

"Well," repeated Valentine, "for all that, and though he referred to that very text, I did not like to hear him say that he blessed God he had been led to do it; and that, if ever I heard of it, I was to remember that he thought of it with gratitude." Saying this, he turned over the pages again. "But there is nothing of that here," he said, "how did you discover it?"

"I was told of it at Melcombe," said Brandon, hesitating.

"By whom?"

"It seemed to be familiarly known there." He glanced at the *Times* which was laid on the table just beyond the desk at which Valentine sat. "It was little Peter Melcombe," he said gravely, "who mentioned it to me."

"What! the poor little heir!" exclaimed Valentine,

rather contemptuously. "I would not be in his shoes for a good deal! But Giles—but Giles—you have shown me the letter!"

He started up.

"Yes, there IT is," said Giles, glancing again at the *Times*, for he perceived instantly that Valentine for the first time had remembered on what contingency he was to be told of this matter.

There it was indeed! The crisis of his fate in a few sorrowful words had come before him.

"At Corfu, on the 28th of February, to the inexpressible grief of his mother, Peter, only child of the late Peter Melcombe, Esq., and great-grandson and heir of the late Mrs. Melcombe, of Melcombe. In the twelfth year of his age."

"Good heavens!" exclaimed Valentine, in an awe-struck whisper. "Then it has come to this, after all?"

He sat silent so long, that his brother had full time once more to consider this subject in all its bearings, to perceive that Valentine was trying to discover some reasonable cause for what his father had done, and then to see his countenance gradually clear and his now flashing eyes lose their troubled expression.

"I know you have respected my poor father's confidence," he said at last.

"Yes, I have."

"And you never heard anything from him by word of mouth that seemed afterwards to connect itself with this affair?"

"Yes, I did," Brandon answered, "he said to me just before my last voyage, that he had written an important letter, told me where it was, and desired me to observe that his faculties were quite unimpaired long after the writing of it."

"I do not think they could have been," Valentine put in, and he continued his questions. "You think that you have never, never heard him say anything, at any time which at all puzzled or startled you, and which you remembered after this?"

"No, I never did. He never surprised me, or excited any suspicion at any time about anything, till I had broken the seal of that letter."

"And after all," Valentine said, turning the pages, "how little there is in it, how little it tells me!"

"Hardly anything, but there is a great deal, there is everything in his having been impelled to write it."

"Well, poor man" (Giles was rather struck by this

epithet), "if secrecy was his object, he has made that at least impossible. I must soon know all, whatever it is. And more than that, if I act as he wishes, in fact, as he commands, all the world will set itself to investigate the reason."

"Yes, I am afraid so," Brandon answered, "I have often thought of that."

Valentine went on. "I always knew, felt rather, that he must have had a tremendous quarrel with his elder brother. He never would mention him if he could help it, and showed an ill-disguised unforgiving sort of—almost dread, I was going to say, of him, as if he had been fearfully bullied by him in his boyhood and could not forget it; but," he continued, still pondering, "it surely is carrying both anger and superstition a little too far, to think that when he is in his grave it will do his son any harm to inherit the land of the brother he quarrelled with."

"Yes," said Giles, "when one considers how most of the land of this country was first acquired, how many crimes lie heavy on its various conquerors, and how many more have been perpetrated in its transmission from one possessor to another;" then he paused, and Valentine took up his words.

"It seems incredible that he should have thought an old quarrel (however bitter) between two boys ought, more than half a century afterwards, to deprive the son of one of them from taking his lawful inheritance."

"Yes," Brandon said. "He was no fool; he could not have thought so, and therefore it could not have been that, or anything like it. Nor could he have felt that he was in any sense answerable for the poor man's death, for I have ascertained that there had been no communication between the two branches of the family for several years before he laid violent hands on himself."

Valentine sighed restlessly. "The whole thing is perfectly unreasonable," he said; "in fact, it would be impossible to do as he desires, even if I were ever so willing."

"Impossible?" exclaimed Brandon.

"Yes, the estate is already mine; how is it possible for me not to take it? I must prove the will, the old will, the law would see to that, for there will be legacy duty to pay. Even if I chose to fling the income into the pond, I must save out enough to satisfy the tax-gatherers. You seem to take for granted that I will and can calmly and secretly let the estate be. But have you thought out the details at all? Have you formed any theory as to how this is to be done?"

He spoke with some impatience and irritation, it vexed him to perceive that his brother had fully counted on the dead father's letter being obeyed. Brandon had nothing to say.

"Besides," continued Valentine, "where is this sort of thing to stop? If I die to-morrow, John is my heir. Is he to let it alone? Could he?"

"I don't know," answered Brandon. "He has not the same temptation to take it that you have."

"Temptation!" repeated Valentine.

Brandon did not retract or explain the word.

"And does he know any reason, I wonder, why he should renounce it?" continued Valentine, but as he spoke his hand, which he had put out to take the *Times*, paused on its way, and his eyes involuntarily opened a little wider. Something, it seemed, had struck him, and he was recalling it and puzzling it out. Two or three lilies thrown under a lilac tree by John's father had come back to report themselves, nothing more recent or more startling than that, for he was still thinking of the elder brother. "And he must have hated him to the full as much as my poor father did," was his thought. "That garden had been shut up for his sake many, many years. Wait a minute, if that man got the estate wrongfully, I'll have nothing to do with it after all. Nonsense! Why do I slander the dead in my thoughts? as if I had not read that will many times—he inherited after the old woman's sickly brother, who died at sea." After this his thoughts wandered into all sorts of vague and intricate paths that led to no certain goal; he was not even certain at last that there was anything real to puzzle about. His father might have been under some delusion after all.

At last his wandering eyes met Brandon's.

"Well!" he exclaimed, as if suddenly waking up.

"How composedly he takes it, and yet how amazed he is!" thought Brandon. "Well," he replied, by way of answer.

"I shall ask you, Giles, as you have kept this matter absolutely secret so long, to keep it secret still; at any rate for awhile, from every person whatever."

"I think you have a right to expect that of me. I will."

"Poor little fellow! died at Corfu then. The news is all over Wigfield by this time, no doubt. John knows it of course, now." Again he paused, and this time it was his uncle's last conversation that recurred to his memory. It was most unwelcome. Brandon could see that he looked more than disturbed; he was also angry; and yet after awhile, both these feelings melted away, he was like a man who had walked up to a cobweb, that stretched itself before his face, but when he had put up his hand and cleared it off, where was it?

He remembered how the vague talk of a dying old man had startled him.

The manner of the gift and the odd feeling he had suffered at the time, as if it might be somehow connected with the words said, appeared to rise up to be looked at. But one can hardly look straight at a thing of that sort without making it change its aspect. Sensations and impressions are subject to us; they may be reasoned down. His reason was stronger than his fear had been, and made it look foolish. He brought back the words, they were disjointed, they accused no one, they could not be put together. So he covered that recollection over, and threw it aside.

He did not consciously hide it from himself, but he did know in his own mind that he should not relate it to his brother.

"Well, you have done your part," he said at length; "and now I must see about doing mine."

"No one could feel more keenly than I do, how hard this is upon you," said Brandon; but Valentine detected a tone of relief in his voice, as if he took the words to mean a submission to the father's wish, and as if he was glad. "My poor father might have placed some confidence in me, instead of treating me like a child," he said bitterly; "why on earth could he not tell me all?"

"Why, my dear fellow," exclaimed Brandon; "surely if you were to renounce the property, it would have been hard upon you and John to be shamed or tortured by any knowledge of the crime and disgrace that it came with."

"'That it came with!" repeated Valentine; "you take that for granted, then? You have got further than I have."

"I think, of course, that the crime was committed, or the disgrace incurred, for the sake of the property."

"Well," said Valentine, "I am much more uncertain about the whole thing than you seem to be. I shall make it my duty to investigate the matter. I must find out everything; perhaps it will be only too easy; according to what I find I shall act. One generation has no right so to dominate over another as to keep it always in childlike bondage to a command for which no reason is given. If, when I know, I consider that my dear father was right, I shall of my own free-will sell the land, and divest myself of the proceeds. If that he was wrong, I shall go and live fearlessly and freely in that house, and on that land which, in the course of providence, has come to me."

"Reasonable and cool," thought Brandon. "Have I any right to say more? He will do just what he says. No one was ever more free from superstition; and he is of age, as he reminds me."

"Very well," he then said aloud; "you have a right to do as you please. Still, I must remind you of your father's distinct assertion, that in this case he has set you an example. He would not have the land."

"Does he mean," said Valentine, confused between

his surprise at the letter, his own recollections, and his secret wishes—"Does he, can he mean, that his old mother positively asked him to be her heir, and he refused?"

"I cannot tell; how is the will worded?"

"My great-grandfather left his estate to his only son, and if *he* died childless, to his eldest grandson; both these were mere boys at the time, and if neither lived to marry, then the old man left his estate to his only daughter. That was my grandmother, you know, and she had it for many years."

"And she had power to will it away, as is evident."

"Yes, she might leave it to any one of her sons, or his representative; but she was not to divide it into shares. And in case of the branch she favoured dying out, the estate was to revert to his heir-at-law— the old man's heir-at-law, you know, his nearest of kin. That would have been my father, if he had lived a year or two longer, he was the second son. It is a most complicated and voluminous will."

Brandon asked one more question. "But its provisions come to an end with you, is it not so? It is not entailed, and you can do with it exactly as you please."

Valentine's countenance fell a little when his brother said this; he perceived that he chanced to be more free than most heirs, he had more freedom than he cared for.

"Yes," he replied, " that is so."

## CHAPTER IX.

### SOPHISTRY.

"'As he has not trusted me, he will never know how I should scorn to be a thief,' quoth the school boy yesterday, when his master's orchard gate was locked; but, 'It's all his own fault,' quoth the same boy to-day while he was stealing his master's plums, 'why did he leave the gate ajar?'"

"VAL," said Brandon, "I do hope you will give yourself time to consider this thing in all its bearings before you decide. I am afraid if you make a mistake, it will prove a momentous one."

He spoke with a certain feeling of restraint, his advice had not been asked; and the two brothers began to perceive by this time that it was hard to keep up an air of easy familiarity when neither felt really at ease. Each was thinking of the lovely young wife down-stairs. One felt that he could hardly preach to the man whose folly had been his own opportunity, the other felt that nothing would be more sweet than to let her see that, after all, she had married a man not half so rich nor in so good a position as her first love, for so he chose to consider himself. How utter, how thorough an escape this would be also from the least fear of further dependence on Giles! And, as to his having made a fool of himself, and having been well laughed at for his pains, he was perfectly aware that as Melcombe of Melcombe, and with those personal advantages that he by no means undervalued, nobody would choose to remember that story against him, and he might marry almost wherever he pleased.

As he turned in his chair to think, he caught a glimpse of his old uncle's house, just a corner through some trees, of his own bedroom window there, the place where that parcel was.

He knew that, think as long as he would, Giles would not interrupt. "Yes, that parcel! Well, I'm independent, anyhow," he considered exultingly; and the further thought came into his mind, "I am well enough off. What if I were to give this up and stay with John? I know he is surprised and pleased to find me so useful. I shall be more so; the work suits me, and brings out all I have in me; I like it. Then I always liked being with Emily, and I should soon be master in that house. Bother the estate! I felt at first that I could not possibly fling it by, but really—really I believe that in a few years, when John goes into Parliament, he'll make me his partner. It's very perplexing; yes, I'll think it well over, as Giles says. I'll do as I please; and I've a great mind to let that doomed old den alone after all."

Though he expressed his mind in these undignified words, it was not without manly earnestness that he turned back to his brother, and said seriously, "Giles, I do assure you that I will decide nothing till I have given the whole thing my very best attention. In the meantime, of course, whatever you hear, you will say nothing. I shall certainly not go to Melcombe for a few days, I've got so attached to John, somehow, that I cannot think of leaving him in the lurch just now when he is out of spirits, and likes to have me with him."

Thereupon the brothers parted, Valentine going downstairs, and Brandon sitting still in his room, a smile dawning on his face, and a laugh following.

"Leaving John in the lurch!" he repeated. "What would my lord John think if he could hear that; but I have noticed for some time that they like one another. What a notion Val has suddenly formed of his own importance! There was really something like dignity in his leave-taking. He does not intend that I should interfere, as is evident. And I am not certain that if he asked for my advice I should know what to say. I was very clear in my own mind that when he consulted me I should say, 'Follow your father's desire.' I am still clear that I would do so myself in such a case; but I am not asked for my opinion. I think he will renounce the inheritance, on reflection; if he does, I shall be truly glad that it was not at all by my advice, or to please me. But if he does not? Well, I shall not wish to make the thing out any worse than it is. I always thought that letter weak as a command, but strong as a warning. It would be, to say the least of it, a dutiful and filial action to respect that warning. A warning not to perpetuate some wrong, for instance; but what wrong? I saw a miniature of Daniel Mortimer the elder, smiling, handsome, and fair-haired. It not only reminded me strongly of my step-father, but of the whole race, John, Valentine, John's children, and all. Therefore, I am sure there need be 'no scandal about Queen Elizabeth' Mortimer, and its discovery on the part of her son."

Meanwhile, Valentine, instead of driving straight back to Wigfield, stopped short at his sister Emily's new house, intending to tell her simply of the death of little Peter Melcombe, and notice how she took it. O that the letter had been left to him instead of to Giles! How difficult it was, moreover, to believe that Giles had possessed it so long, and yet that its contents were dead to every one else that breathed! If Giles had not shown him by his manner what he ought to do, he thought he might have felt better inclined to do it. Certain it is that being now alone, he thought of his father's desire with more respect.

Emily had been settled about a month in her new house, and Miss Christie Grant was with her. There was a pretty drawing-room, with bow windows at the back of it. Emily had put there her Indian cabinets, and many other beautiful things brought from the east, besides decorating it with delicate ferns, and bulbs in flower. She was slightly inclined to be lavish so far as she could afford it; but her Scotch blood kept her just on the right side of prudence, and so gave more grace to her undoubted generosity.

This house, which had been chosen by Mrs. Henfrey, was less than a quarter of a mile from John

Mortimer's, and was approached by the same sandy lane. In front, on the opposite side of this lane, the house was sheltered by a great cliff, crowned with fir trees, and enriched with wild plants and swallows' caves; and behind, at the end of her garden, ran the same wide brook which made a boundary for John Mortimer's ground.

This circumstance was a great advantage to the little Mortimers, who with familiar friendship made themselves at once at home all over Mrs. Nemily's premises, and forthwith set little boats and ships afloat on the brook in the happy certainty that sooner or later they would come down to their rightful owners.

Valentine entered the drawing-room, and a glance as he stooped to kiss his sister served to assure him that she knew nothing of the great news.

She put her two hands upon his shoulders, and her sweet eyes looked into his. A slightly shamefaced expression struck her. "Does the dear boy think he is in love again?" she thought; "who is it, I wonder?" The look became almost sheepish; and she, rather surprised, said to him, "Well, Val, you see the house is ready."

"Yes," he answered, looking round him with a sigh.

Emily felt that he might well look grave and sad; it was no common friend that he had lost. "How is John?" she asked.

"Why, he was very dull, very dull indeed, when I left him this morning; and natural enough he should be."

"Yes, most natural."

Then he said, after a little more conversation on their recent loss, "Emily, I came to tell you something very important—to me at least," here the shame-faced look came back. "Oh, no," he exclaimed, as a flash of amazement leaped out of her eyes; "nothing of that sort."

"I am glad to hear it," she answered, not able to forbear smiling; "but sit down then, you great, long-legged fellow, you put me out of conceit with this room; you make the ceiling look too low."

"Oh, do I?" said Valentine, and he sat down in a comfortable chair, and thought he could have been very happy with Emily, and did not know how to begin to tell her.

"I must say I admire your taste, Emily," he then

said, looking about him, and shirking the great subject.

Emily was a little surprised at his holding off in this way, so she in her turn took the opportunity to say something fresh; something that she thought he might as well hear.

"And so John's dull, is he? Poor John! Do you know, Val, the last time I saw him he was very cross."

"Indeed! why was he cross?"

"It was about a month ago. He laughed, but I know he was cross. St. George and I went over at his breakfast-time to get the key of this house, which had been left with him; and, while I ran up-stairs to see the children, he told St. George how, drawing up his blind to shave that morning, he had seen you chasing Barbara and Miss Green (that little temporary governess of theirs) about the garden. Barbara threw some snowballs at you, but you caught her and kissed her."

"She is a kind of cousin," Valentine murmured; "besides, she is a mere child."

"But she is a very tall child," said Emily. "She is within two inches as tall as I am. Miss Green is certainly no child."

Valentine did not wish to enter on that side of the question. "I'm sure I don't know how one can find out when to leave off kissing one's cousins," he observed.

"Oh! I can give you an easy rule for that," said Emily; "leave off the moment you begin to care to do it: they will probably help you by beginning, just about the same time, to think they have bestowed kisses enough."

"It all arose out of my kindness," said Valentine. "John had already begun to be anxious about the dear old man, so I went over that morning before breakfast, and sent him up a message. His father was decidedly better; and as he had to take a journey that day, I thought he should know it as soon as possible. But Emily——"

"Yes, dear boy?"

"I really did come to say something important." And instantly as he spoke he felt what a tragical circumstance this was for some one else, and that such would be Emily's first thought and view of it.

"What is it?" she exclaimed, now a little startled.

Valentine had turned rather pale. He tasted the bitter ingredients in this cup of prosperity more plainly now; and he wished that letter was at the bottom of the sea. "Why—why it is something you will be very sorry for, too," he said, his voice faltering. "It's poor little Peter Melcombe."

"Oh!" exclaimed Emily, with an awestruck shudder. "There! I said so."

"WHAT did you say?" cried Valentine, so much struck by her words that he recovered his self-possession instantly.

"Poor, poor woman," she went on, the ready tears falling on her cheeks; "and he was her only child!"

"But what do you mean, Emily?" continued Valentine, startled and suspicious. "*What* did you say?"

"Oh!" she answered, "nothing that I had any particular reason for saying. I felt that it might be a great risk to take that delicate boy to Italy again, where he had been ill before, and I told John I wished we could prevent it. I could not forget that his death would be a fine thing for my brother, and I felt a sort of fear that this would be the end of it."

Valentine was relieved. She evidently knew nothing, and he could listen calmly while she went on.

"My mere sense of the danger made it a necessity

for me to act. I suppose you will be surprised when I tell you"—here two more tears fell—"that I wrote to Mrs. Melcombe. I knew she was determined to go on the Continent, and I said if she liked to leave her boy behind, I would take charge of him. It was the day before dear Fred was taken ill."

"And she declined!" said Valentine. "Well, it was very kind of you, very good of you, and just like you. Let us hope poor Mrs. Melcombe does not remember it now."

"Yes, she declined; said her boy had an excellent constitution. Where did the poor little fellow die?"

"At Corfu."

Emily wept for sympathy with the mother, and Valentine sat still opposite to her, and was glad of the silence; it pleased him to think of this that Emily had done, till all on a sudden some familiar words out of the Bible flashed into his mind, strange, quaint words, and it seemed much more as if somebody kept repeating them in his presence than as if he had turned them over himself to the surface, from among the mass of scraps that were lying littered about in the chambers of his memory. "'The words of Jonadab the son of Rechab, that he commanded his sons."

"May I see the letter?" asked Emily.

"There was no letter; we saw it in the *Times*," said Valentine; and again the mental repetition began. "The son of Rechab, that he commanded HIS sons, are performed; for unto this day——"

Emily had dried her eyes now. "Well, Val dear," she said, and hesitated.

"Oh, I wish she would give me time to get once straight through to the end, and have done with it," thought Valentine. "'The words of Jonadab the son of Rechab, that he commanded *his* sons, are——' (yes, only the point of it is that they're not—not yet, at any rate) the words of Jonadab."

Here Emily spoke again. "Well, Val, nobody ever came into an estate more naturally and rightly than you do, for, however well you may have behaved about it, and nobody could have behaved better, you must have felt that as the old lady chose to leave all to one son, that should not have been the youngest. I hope you will be happy; and I know you will make a kind, good landlord. It seems quite providential that you should have spent so much time in learning all about land and farming. I have always felt that all which was best and nicest in you would come out, if you could have prosperity, and we now see that it was intended for you."

Cordial, delightful words to Valentine; they almost made him forget this letter that she had never heard of.

"Oh, if you please, ma'am," exclaimed a female servant, bursting into the room, "Mr. Brandon's love to you. He has sent the pony-carriage, and he wants you to come back in it directly."

Something in the instant attention paid to this message, and the alacrity with which Emily ran up-stairs, as if perfectly ready, and expectant of it, showed Valentine that it did not concern his inheritance. but also what and whom it probably did concern, and he sauntered into the little hall to wait for Emily, put her into the carriage and fold the rug round her, while he observed without much surprise that she had for the moment quite forgotten his special affairs, and was anxious and rather urgent to be off.

Then he drove into Wigfield, considering in his own mind that if John did not know anything concerning the command in this strange letter, he and he only was the person who ought to be told and consulted about it.

It rained now, and when he entered the bank and paused to take off his wet coat, he saw on every face as it was lifted up that his news was known, and his heart beat so fast as he knocked at John's door that he had hardly strength to obey the hearty "Come in."

Two minutes would decide what John knew, and whether he also had a message to give him from the dead. John was standing with his back to the fire, grave and lost in thought. Valentine came in, and sat down on one side of the grate, putting his feet on the fender to warm them. When he had done this, he longed to change his attitude, for John neither moved nor spoke, and he could not see his face. His own agitation made him feel that he was watched, and that he could not seem ill at ease, and must not be the first to move; but at last when the silence and immobility of John became intolerable to him, he suddenly pushed back his chair, and looked up. John then turned his head slightly, and their eyes met.

"You know it," said Valentine.

"Yes," John answered gravely, "of course."

"Oh! what next, what next?" thought Valentine, and he spent two or three minutes in such a tumult of keen expectation and eager excitement, that he could hear every beat of his heart quite plainly, and then—

"It is a very great upset of all my plans," John said, still with more gravity than usual. "I had fully intended—indeed, I had hoped, old fellow, that you and I would be partners some day."

"Oh, John," exclaimed Valentine, a sudden revulsion of feeling almost overcoming him now he found that his fears as to what John might be thinking of were groundless. "Oh, John, I wish we could! It might be a great deal better for me. And so you really did mean it? You are more like a brother than anything else. I hate the thought of that ill-starred house; I think I'll stop here with you."

"Nonsense," said John, just as composedly and as gravely as ever; "what do you mean, you foolish lad?" But he appreciated the affection Valentine had expressed for him, and kindly put his hand on his young relative's shoulder.

Valentine had never found it so hard to understand himself as at that moment. His course was free,

Giles could not speak, and John knew nothing; yet either the firm clasp of a man's hand on his shoulder roused him to the fact that he cared for this man so much that he could be happier under his orders than free and his own master, or else his father's words gathered force by mere withdrawal of opposition.

For a moment he almost wished John did know; he wanted to be fortified in his desire to remain with him; and yet—— No! he could not tell him; that would be taking his fate out of his own hands for ever.

"You think then I must—take it up; in short, go and live in it?" he said at length.

"Think!" exclaimed John, with energy and vehemence; "why, who could possibly think otherwise?"

"I've always been accustomed to go in and out amongst a posse of my own relations."

"Your own relations must come to you then," answered John pleasantly, "I, for one. Why, Melcombe's only fifty or sixty miles off, man!"

"It seems to me now that I'm very sorry for that poor little fellow's death," Valentine went on.

"Nobody could have behaved better during his

lifetime than you have done," John said. "Why, Val," he exclaimed, looking down, "you astonish me!"

Valentine was vainly struggling with tears. John went and bolted the door; then got some wine, and brought him a glass.

"As calm as possible during my father's death and funeral," he thought, "and now half choking himself, forsooth, because his fortune's made, and he must leave his relations. I trust and hope, with all my heart, that Dorothea is not at the bottom of this! I supposed his nerves to be strong enough for anything."

Valentine was deadly pale. He put up a shaking hand for the glass, and as he drank the wine, and felt the blood creeping warmly about his limbs again, he thought "John knows nothing whatever. No wonder he is astonished, he little thinks what a leap in the dark it is."

And so the die was cast.

A few days after this Gladys and Barbara received letters; the first ran as follows:—

"MY DEAR YOUNG FRIENDS,—Owe you three-and-sixpence for Blob's biscuits, do I? Don't you know that it is not polite to remind people of their debts? When you would have been paid that money I cannot think, if it were not for a circumstance detailed below. I have just been reading that the finest minds always possess a keen sense of humour, so if you find nothing to laugh at in this, it will prove that there is nothing particular in you. Did I ever think there was? Well, why *will* you ask such awkward questions?—Off!

### THE NOBLE TUCK-MAN.

Americus as he did wend
   With A. J. Mortimer, his chum,
The two were greeted by a friend,
   "And how are you, boys, Hi, Ho, Hum?"

He spread a note so crisp, so neat
   (Ho and Hi, and tender Hum),
"If you of this a fifth can eat
   I'll give you the remainder. Come!"

To the tuck-shop three repair
   (Ho and Hum, and pensive Hi),
One looks on to see all's fair
   Two call out for hot mince pie.

Thirteen tarts, a few Bath buns
   (Hi and Hum, and gorgeous Ho),
Lobster cakes (the butter'd ones),
   All at once they cry "No go."

Then doth tuck-man smile. "Them there
   (Ho and Hi, and futile Hum)
Jellies three and sixpence air,
   Use of spoons an equal sum."

Three are rich. Sweet task 'tis o'er,
   "Tuckman, you're a brick," they cry,
Wildly then shake hands all four
   (Hum and Ho, the end is Hi).

"N.B.—He spoke as good English as we did, and we did not shake hands with him. Such is poetic license. I may have exaggerated a little, as to the number of things we ate. I repeat, I *may* have done. You will never be able to appreciate me till you have learned to make allowance for such little eccentricities of genius.

"Yours, with sentiments that would do anybody credit,

"GIFFORD CRAYSHAW."

The second letter, which was also addressed to both sisters, was from Johnnie, and ran as follows:—

"Now look here, you two fellows are not to expect me to spend all my spare time in writing to you. Where do you think I am now? Why, at Brighton.

"Val's a brick. Yesterday was our *Exeat*, and he came down to Harrow, called for me and Cray, and brought us here to the Old Ship Hotel. We two chose the dinner, and in twenty minutes that dinner was gone like a dream. Val and Cray made the unlucky waiter laugh till he dropped the butter-boat. The waiter was a proud man—I never saw a prouder.

He had made up his mind that nothing should make him laugh, but at last we had him. Beware of pride, my friends.

"Then we went to the Aquarium. My wig! I never saw anything so extraordinary. It ought to be called the Aquaria, for there are dozens of them. They are like large rooms full of water, and you go and look in at the fish through the windows. No, they're more like caves than rooms, they have rocks for walls. Talk of the ancient Greeks! I'll never wish to be one of those fogies again! I've seen turtles now under water, sitting opposite to one another, bowing and looking each in his fellow's face, just like two cats on a rug. Why the world's full of things that *they* knew nothing about.

"But I had no notion that fish were such fools, some of them, at least. There were some conger eels seven feet long, and when we stared at them they went and stuck their little heads into crevices in the rocks. I should like to have reasoned with them, for they evidently thought they were hidden, while, in fact, they were wriggling upside down, full in view. Well, so then we went to see the octopus. One was just like a pink satin bag, covered with large ivory buttons, but that was only because it was inside out. While I was watching it I rather started, for I saw in a corner of the den close to me an enormous sort of bloated sea toadstool (as I thought), but it had eyes, it was covered with warts, it seemed very faint, and it heaved and panted. By that time a conglomeration like a mass of writhing serpents was letting itself down the side of the den, and when it got to the bottom it shot out a head, made itself into the exact shape of an owl without wings, and began to fly about the place. That made three.

"An old woman who was looking at them too, called out then, 'Oh, you brute, I hate you,' and Val said to her, 'My good lady, allow me to suggest that it is not hatred you feel, but envy. Envy is a very bad passion, and it is our duty to try and restrain it.' 'Sir,' said the old lady, rather fiercely. 'No, we must not give way to envy,' Val persisted, 'though, indeed, what are we in comparison with creatures who can turn themselves inside out as soon as look at you, fly without wings, and walk up a precipice by means of one pearl button?' 'If the police were after you, it might be handy to turn yourself inside out, I'll allow,' she answered, in a very loud, angry voice, 'so as they should not know you; but I wouldn't, if I could, I'll assure you, young man, no, that I wouldn't, not for all the pearl buttons in the world.'

"Well, I never wrote such a long letter in my life, it must count for three, mind. We had a great deal more fun after that, but Val and I got away, because a little crowd collected. Cray stayed behind, pretending he did not belong to us, and he heard a man say, 'Perhaps the gentleman's a parson; that sort always think they ought to be *moralising* about something or other.' And he found out by their talk that the old lady was a clearstarcher, so when she was alone again we went back. Val said he should be some time at Brighton, and he gave her his address and offered her his washing. She asked for his name, too, and he replied—you know how grave Val is—'Well, ma'am, I'm sorry to say I cannot oblige you with my name, because I don't know it. All I am sure about is, that it begins with an M; but I've written up to London, and I shall know for a certainty the week after next.' So she winked at me, and tapped herself on the forehead. Val is very much vexed because he came up to

London about the will, and the lawyers say he cannot —or somebody else, I don't know which—cannot administer it unless he takes the name of Melcombe. So what he said was quite true, and afterwards we heard the old lady telling her friends that he was demented, but he seemed very harmless and good.

"It's an extraordinary thing, isn't it, that Val has turned out to be rich. Please thank father for writing and telling me about it all. Val doesn't seem to care, and he hates changing his name. He was quite crusty when we congratulated him.

"Give my love to the kids, and tell them if they don't weed my garden they will catch it when I come home.

"I remain, your deservedly revered brother,

"A. J. M."

A postscript followed, from Crayshaw :—

"What this fellow says is quite right, our letters are worth three of yours. You never once mentioned my guinea-pigs in your last, and we don't care whether there is a baby at Wigfield or not. Pretty, is he?

I know better, they are all ugly. Fanny Crayshaw has just got another. I detest babies; but George thinks (indeed many parents do) that the youngest infant is just as much a human being as he is himself, even when it is squalling, in fact more so."

## CHAPTER X.

### DANTE AND OTHERS.

"He climbed the wall of heaven, and saw his love
Safe at her singing; and he left his foes
In vales of shadow weltering, unassoiled,
Immortal sufferers henceforth, in both worlds."

IT was the middle of April. Valentine was gone, and the Mortimer children were running wild, for their nurse had suddenly departed on account of the airs of the new lady-housekeeper, who, moreover, had quarrelled with the new governess.

John was now without doubt Mr. Mortimer, the head of his family and all alone of his name, for Valentine had been obliged to take the name of Melcombe, and, rather to the surprise of his family, had no sooner got things a little settled than he had started across the Continent to meet Mrs. Peter Melcombe, and bring her home to England.

Mr. Mortimer still felt his father's death, and he regretted Valentine's absence more than he cared to confess. He lost his temper rather often, at that particular season, for he did not know where to turn. The housekeeper and the governess insisted frequently on appealing to him against each other, about all sorts of matters that he knew nothing of, and the children took advantage of their feuds to do precisely as they pleased. John's house, though it showed evidently enough that it was a rich man's abode, had a comfortable homeliness about it, but it had always been a costly house to keep; and now that it was less than ever needful to him to save money, he did not want to hear recriminations concerning such petty matters as the too frequent tuning of the school-room piano, and the unprofitable fabrics which had been bought for the children's dresses.

In less than two years Parliament would dissolve. It was now frequently said that Mr. Mortimer was to stand for the borough of Wigfield; but how this was compatible with the present state of his household he did not know.

"I suppose," he said to himself one morning, with a mighty sigh, "I suppose there is only one way out of it all. I really must take a liking to red hair. Well! not just yet."

It was about ten o'clock in the morning when he said this, and he was setting out to walk across the fields, and call for the first time on Mrs. Frederic Walker. He was taking his three younger children with him to make an apology to her.

Now that Mrs. Walker was a widow, she and Mr. Mortimer had half unconsciously changed their manner slightly towards each other; they were just as friendly as before, but not so familiar; the children, however, were very intimate with her.

"She didn't want that bit of garden," argued little Hugh, as one who felt aggrieved; "and when she saw that we had taken it she only laughed."

The fact was, that finding a small piece of waste ground at the back of Mrs. Walker's shrubbery, the children had dug it over, divided it with oyster-shells into four portions, planted it with bulbs and roots, and in their own opinion it was now theirs. They came rather frequently to dig in it. Sometimes on these occasions they went in-doors to see " Mrs. Nemily," and perhaps partake of bread and jam. Once they came in to complain of her gardener, who had been weeding in *their* gardens. They wished her to forbid this. Emily laughed, and said she would.

Their course of honest industry was, however, discovered at last by the twins; and now they were to give up the gardens, which seemed a sad pity, just when they had been intending to put in spring crops.

Some people never really *have* anything. It is not only that they can get no good out of things (that is common even among those who are able both to have and to hold), but that they don't know how to reign over their possessions and appropriate them.

Their chattels appear to know this, and despise them; their dogs run after other men; the best branches of their rose-trees climb over the garden-wall, and people who smell at the flowers there appear to supply a reason for any roses being planted inside. Such people always know their weak point, and spend their own money as if they had stolen it.

The little Mortimers were not related to them. Here was a piece of ground which nobody cultivated; it manifestly wanted owners; they took it, weeded it, and flung out all the weeds into Mrs. Walker's garden.

The morning was warm; a south wind was fluttering the half-unfolded leaf-buds, and spreading abroad the soft odour of violets and primroses which covered the sunny slopes.

John's children, when they came in at Mrs. Walker's drawing-room window, brought some of this delicate fragrance of the spring upon their hair and clothes. Grown-up people are not in the habit of rolling about, or tumbling down over beds of flowers. They must take the consequences, and leave the ambrosial scents of the wood behind them.

John himself, who had not been prepared to see them run off from him at the last moment, beheld their active little legs disappearing as they got over the low ledge of the open window. He, however, did not follow their example, but walked round to the front of the house, and was shown into the drawing-room, after ringing the bell, Emily lifting up her head at his entrance with evident surprise. He was surprised too, even startled, for on a sofa opposite to her sat a lady whom he had been thinking of a good deal during the previous month—her of the golden head, Miss Justina Fairbairn. It was evident that the children had not announced his intended call.

Miss Justina Fairbairn was the daughter of an old

K.C.B. deceased. She and her mother were poor, but they were much respected as sensible, dignified women; and they had that kind of good opinion of themselves which those who hold in sincerity (having no doubt or misgiving) can generally spread among their friends.

Miss Fairbairn was a fine, tall woman, with something composed and even motherly in her appearance; her fair and rather wide face had a satisfied, calm expression, excepting when she chanced to meet John, and then a flash would come from those cold blue eyes, a certain hope, doubt, or feeling of suspense would assert itself in spite of her. It never rose to actual expectation, for she was most reasonable; and John had never shown her any attention; but she had a sincere conviction that a marriage with her would be the best and most suitable that was possible for him. It was almost inconceivable, she thought, that he could escape the knowledge of this fact long. She was so every way suitable. She was about thirty-two years of age, and she felt sure he ought not to marry a younger woman.

Many people thought as she did, that Mr. Mortimer could not do better than marry Miss Fairbairn;

and it is highly probable that this opinion had originated with herself, though it must be well understood that she had not expressed it. Thoughts are certainly able to spread themselves without the aid of looks or language. Invisible seed that floats from the parent plant can root itself wherever it settles; and thoughts must have some medium through which they sail till they reach minds that can take them in, and there they strike root, and whole crops of the same sort come up, just as if they were indigenous, and naturally belonging to their entertainers. This is even more true in great matters than in small.

Miss Fairbairn, as usual when she saw John, became gracious. John was thought to be a very intellectual man; she was intellectual, and meant to be more so. John was specially fond of his children; her talk concerning children should be both wise and kind.

Real love of children and childhood is, however, a quality that no one can successfully feign. John had occasionally been seen, by observant matrons and maids, to attempt with a certain uncouth tenderness to do his children womanly service. He could tie their bonnet-strings and sashes when these came undone. They had been known to apply to him during a walk to take stones out of their boots, and also to lace these up again.

Why should we write of children as if they were just like grown-up people? They are not in the least like, any more than they are like one another; but here they are, and if we can neither love nor understand them, woe betide us!

"No more crying, my dear," John had said that morning to his youngest daughter.

He had just administered a reproof to her as he sat a breakfast, for some infantile delinquency; and she, sniffing and sobbing piteously, testified a desire to kiss him in token of penitence.

"I'm good now," she remarked.

"Where's your pocket-handkerchief?" said her father, with magisterial dignity.

The infant replied that she had lost it, and straight-way asked to borrow his.

John lent the article, and having made use of it, she pushed it back with all good faith into his breast-pocket, and repeating, "I'm good now," received the coveted kiss, and presently after a donation of buttered toast, upon which she became as happy as ever.

In ordinary life it devolves on the mother to lend a handkerchief; but if children have none, there are fathers who can rise to such occasions, and not feel afterwards as if heroic sacrifices had been demanded of them.

John Mortimer felt that Miss Fairbairn had never before greeted him with so much *empressement*. They sat down, and she immediately began to talk to him. A flattering hope that he had known of her presence and had come at once to see her, gave her just the degree of excitement that she wanted to enable her to produce her thoughts at their best; while he, accustomed by experience to caution, and not ready yet to commit himself, longed to remark that he had been surprised as well as pleased to see her. But he found no opportunity at first to do it; and in the meantime Emily sat and looked on, and listened to their conversation with an air of easy *insouciance* very natural and becoming to her. Emily was seven-and-twenty, and had always been accustomed to defer to Miss Fairbairn as much older as well as wiser than herself; and this deference did not seem out o place, for the large, fair spinster made the young matron look slender and girlish.

John Mortimer remembered how Emily had said a year ago that he could not do better than marry Justina. He thought she had invited her there to that end; and as he talked he took care to express to her by looks his good-humoured defiance; whereupon she defended herself with her eyes, and punished him by saying—

"I thought you would come to-day perhaps and see my little house. Do you like it, John? I have been in it less than three months, and I am already quite attached to it. Miss Fairbairn only came last night, and she is delighted with it."

"Yes," said Justina, "I only came last night;" and an air of irrepressible satisfaction spread itself over her face—that Mr. Mortimer should have walked over to see her this very first morning was beyond her utmost hopes. She had caused Emily to invite her at that particular time that she might often see John, and here he was.

"Emily thinks it a pointed thing, my coming at once," he cogitated. "She reminds me, too, that friendship for her did not bring me. Well,

I was too much out of spirits to come a month ago."

Emily's eyes flashed and softened when she saw him out of countenance, and a little twist came in her lips where a smile would like to have broken through. She was still in crape, and wore the delicate gossamer of her widow's cap, with long, wing-like streamers falling away at her back; and while she sat at work on a cumbersome knitted shawl she listened with an air of docility to Justina's conversation, without noticing that a touch of dismay was beginning to show itself in John's face; for Miss Fairbairn had begun to speak of Italian literature, a subject she had been getting up lately for certain good reasons of her own. She dared to talk about Dante, and John was almost at once keenly aware that all this learning was sham—it was the outcome of no real taste; and he felt like a fool while one of the ladies did the wooing and the other, as he thought, amused herself with watching it. He was accustomed to be wooed, and to be watched, but he had been trying for some time to bring his mind to like the present wooer. While away from her he fancied that he had begun to succeed, and now he knew well that this sort of talk would drive him wild in a week. It represented nothing real. No; the thing would not do. She was a good woman; she would have ruled his house well; she would have been just to his children; and if he had established her in all comfort and elegance over his family, he might have left her, and attended to those prospective Parliamentary duties as long as he liked, without annoying her. She was a lady too, and her mother, old Lady Fairbairn, was a pleasant and unexceptionable woman. But she was making herself ridiculous now. No; it would not do.

Giving her up then and there, he suddenly started from his seat as if he felt relieved, and drawing himself to his full height, looked down on the two ladies, one of whom, lifting her golden head, continued the wooing with her eyes, while the other said carelessly and with a dispassionate air—

"Well, I cannot think how you or John or any one can like that bitter-hearted, odious, cruel Dante."

"Emily," exclaimed Miss Fairbairn, "how can you be so absurd, dear?"

"I wonder they did not tear him into little bits," continued Emily audaciously, "instead of merely banishing him, which was all they did—wasn't it, John?"

"I cannot imagine what you mean," exclaimed Miss Fairbairn, while John laughed, and felt that at least here was something real and natural.

"You cannot? That's because you don't consider, then, what we should feel if somebody now were to write a grand poem about our fathers, mothers, aunts, uncles, and dear friends deceased, setting forth how he had seen them all in the nether regions; how he had received their confidences, and how penitent most of them were. Persecuted, indeed! and misunderstood! I consider that his was the deadliest revenge any man ever took upon his enemies."

Miss Fairbairn's brow, on hearing this, contracted with pain; for John laughed again, and turning slightly towards Emily as he stood leaning against the window-frame, took the opportunity to get away from the subject of Italian literature, and ask her some question about her knitting.

"It must be something to give away, I am sure. You are always giving."

"But you know, John," she answered, as if excusing herself, "we are not at all sure that we shall have any possessions, anything of our own, in the future life—anything, consequently, to give away. Perhaps it will all belong to all. So let us have enough of giving while we can, and enjoy the best part of possession."

"Dear Emily," said Miss Fairbairn kindly, "you should not indulge in these unauthorised fancies."

"But it so chances that this is not for a poor person," observed Emily, "but for dear Aunt Christie."

"Ah, she was always very well while she lived with me," said John; "but I hear a very different account of her now."

"Yes; she has rheumatism in her foot; so that she is obliged to sit up-stairs. John, you should go and see her."

"I will take Mr. Mortimer to her," said Justina, rising serenely. This she thought would break off the conversation, in which she had no part.

So John went up to Miss Christie's little sitting-room, and there she was, bolt upright, with her lame foot on a cushion. By this visit he gave unmixed pleasure to the old lady, and afforded opportunity to the younger one for some pleasant, reasonable speeches, and for a little effective waiting on the invalid, as well as for some covert compliments.

"Ay, John Mortimer," quoth Miss Christie, with an audacious twinkle in her eyes, "I'm no that clear that I don't deserve all the pain I've got for my sins against ye."

"Against me!" exclaimed John, amazed.

"Some very bad advice I gave ye, John," she continued, while Miss Fairbairn, a little surprised, looked on.

"Make your mind easy," John answered with mock gravity, for he knew well enough what she meant. "I never follow bad advice. I promise not to follow yours."

"What was your advice, dear?" asked Miss Fairbairn sweetly, her golden head within a yard of John's as she stooped forward. "I wonder you should have ventured to give advice to such a man as Mr. Mortimer. People always seem to think that in any matter of consequence they are lucky if they can get advice from him."

John drew a long breath, and experienced a strong sense of compunction; but Miss Christie was merely relieved, and she began to talk with deep interest about the new governess and the new housekeeper.

Miss Fairbairn brought John down again as soon as she could, and took the opportunity to engage his attention on the stairs, by asking him a question on some political subject that really interested him; and he, like a straightforward man, falling into the trap, began to give her his views respecting it.

But as he opened the drawing-room door for her, his three children, who all this time had been in the garden, came running in at the window, and before he and Miss Fairbairn were seated, his two little boys, treading on Mrs. Walker's crape, were thrusting some large handfuls of flowers almost into her face, while Anastasia emptied a lapful on to her knees. Emily accepted them graciously.

"And so," little Hugh exclaimed, "as father said we were not to have the gardens, we thought we had better gather all the flowers, because *they* are our own, you know," he proceeded; "for we bought most of the bulbs with our own money; and they're all for you."

Hyacinths, narcissus, wallflowers, polyanthus, they continued to be held up for her inspection.

"And you'll let us put them in water ourselves, won't you?" said Bertram.

"Yes, she will, Bertie," cried Hugh.

"Don't tread on Mrs. Walker's dress," John began, and the sprites, as if in ready obedience, were off in an instant; but in reality they were gone to find vases for the flowers, Emily looking up with all composure, though a good deal of scrambling and arguing were heard through the open door.

"We found these in the pantry," exclaimed the two little boys, returning, each with a dish in his hand. "Nancy wanted to get some water, but we wouldn't let her."

"Come here," exclaimed John with gravity; "come here, and shut the door. Emily, I brought these imps on purpose to apologize for their high misdemeanours."

Thereupon the two little boys blushed and hung their heads. It was nothing to have taken the garden, but it daunted them to have to acknowledge the fault. Before they had said a word, however, a shrill little voice cried out behind them—

"But I can't do my *apologize* yet, father, because I've got a pin in my cape, and it pricks, and somebody must take it out."

"I cannot get the least pretence of penitence out of any one of them," exclaimed John, unable to forbear laughing. "I must make the apology myself, Emily. I am very much afraid that these gardens were taken without leave; they were not given at all."

"I have heard you say more than once," answered Emily, with an easy smile, "that it is the privilege of the giver to forget. I never had a very good memory."

"But they confessed themselves that they *took* them."

"Well, John, then if you said they were to apologize," answered Emily, giving them just the shadow of a smile, "of course they must;" and so they did, the little boys with hot blushes and flashing eyes, the little girl with innocent unconsciousness of shame. Then "Mrs. Nemily" rather spoilt the dignity of the occasion by taking her up and kissing her; upon which the child inquired in a loud whisper—

"But now we've done our *apologize*, we may keep our gardens, mayn't we?"

At this neither she nor John could help laughing.

"You may, if papa has no objection," said Emily,

suddenly aware of a certain set look about Miss Fairbairn's lips, and a glance of reproof, almost of anguish, from her stern blue eye.

Miss Fairbairn had that morning tasted the sweetness of hope, and she now experienced a sharp pang of jealousy when she saw the children hanging about Emily with familiar friendliness, treading on her tucks, whispering confidences in her ears, and putting their flowers on the clean chintz of her ottomans. These things Justina would have found intolerable if done to herself, unless in their father's presence. Even then she would have only welcomed them for the sake of diverting them from Emily.

She felt sure that at first all had been as she hoped, and as it ought to be; and she could not refrain from darting a glance of reproof at Emily. She even felt as if it was wrong of John to be thus beguiled into turning away when he ought to have been cultivating his acquaintance with her mind and character. It was still more wrong of Emily to be attracting his notice and drawing him away from his true place, his interest, and now almost his duty.

Emily, with instant docility, put the little Anastasia down and took up her knitting, while Miss Fairbairn, suddenly feigning a great interest in horticulture, asked after John's old gardener, who she heard had just taken another prize.

"The old man is very well," said John, "and if you and Mrs. Walker would come over some morning, I am sure he would be proud to show you the flowers."

Miss Fairbairn instantly accepted the proposal.

"I always took an interest in that old man," she observed; "he is so original."

"Yes, he is," said John.

"But at what time of day are you generally at home," she continued, not observing, or perhaps not intending to observe that the flowers could have been shown during their owner's absence. "At luncheon time, or at what time?"

John, thus appealed to, paused an instant; he had never thought of coming home to entertain the ladies, but he could not be inhospitable, and he concluded that the mistake was real. "At luncheon time," he presently said, and named a day when he would be at home, being very careful to address the invitation to Mrs. Walker.

He then retired with his children, who were now

in very good spirits; they gave their hands to Justina, who would have liked to kiss them, but the sprites skipped away in their father's wake, and while he walked home, lost in thought on grave and serious things, they broke in every now and then with their childish speculations on life and manners.

"Swanny must put on his Sunday coat when they come, and his orange handkerchief that Janie hemmed for him because Mrs. Swan's fingers are all crumpled up," said the little girl.

"Father, what's a Methodist?" asked Hugh.

Before John could answer little Bertram informed his brother, "It is a thing about not going to church. It has nothing to do with her fingers being crumpled up, that's rheumatism."

## CHAPTER XI.

### SELF-WONDER AND SELF-SCORN.

*" Something there is moves me to love, and I
Do know I love, but know not how, nor why."*
A. BROME.

AS John and his children withdrew together through the garden, Justina Fairbairn sat with her work on her knees, watching them.

"Mr. Mortimer is six-and-thirty, is he not?" she asked.

"Yes," answered Emily.

"How much he improves in appearance!" she observed; "he used not to be thought handsome when he was very young—he is both handsome and stately now."

"It is the way with the Mortimers, I think," said Emily. "I should not wonder if in ten years' time Val is just as majestic as the old men used to be, though he has no dignity at all about him now."

"Yes, majesty is the right word," said Justina

## SELF-WONDER AND SELF-SCORN. 215

serenely. "Mr. Mortimer has a finer presence, a finer carriage than formerly; it may be partly because he is not so very thin as he used to be."

"Perhaps so," said Emily.

"And this was his first call," continued Justina, obliged to make openings for herself through which to push what she had to say. "I suppose, dear, you could hardly fail to notice how matters were going. This calling at once, and his bringing the children too; and his wish to find out my opinions, and tell me his own on various subjects."

Silence on the part of the hostess.

"I could almost have wished, dear Emily, that you had not——"

She paused. "Had not what?" asked Emily.

Miss Fairbairn remembered that she was Mrs. Walker's guest, and that it behoved her not to offend her hostess, because she wanted to stay in that house as long as possible. She would like to have finished her speech thus: "that you had not engrossed the children so completely;" but she said instead, with a little smile meant to look conscious, "I believe I meant, dear, that I should have been very glad to talk to the children myself."

She felt that this reply fell rather flat, but she knew that Emily must immediately be made aware of what she now hoped was really the state of the case, and must also be made to help her.

No surprise was expressed, but Mrs. Walker did not make any reply whatever, so she continued,—

"You look surprised, dear, but surely what I have hinted at cannot be a new thought to you," and as it did not suit her to drop the subject yet, she proceeded. "No, I see by your smile that it is not. I confess I should have liked to talk to them, for," she added, with a sigh of contentment, "the task, I see very plainly before me, is always a difficult one to undertake."

Still Emily was silent; she seemed lost in thought; indeed, she was considering among other things that it was little more than a year since she and John had discussed Justina together; was there, could there really be, anything between them now?

Justina watched her, and wished she could know what effect these hints had taken. Emily had always behaved in such a high-minded, noble way to her lovers, and been so generous to other women, that Justina depended on her now. The lower nature paid homage to the higher, even to the point of believing in a sense of honour quite alien to its own experience. There was not the least reason to suppose that Emily cared about John Mortimer, but she wanted her to stand aside lest he should take it into his head to begin to care for her. So many men had been infatuated about Emily, but Emily had never wished to rob another woman for the mere vanity of spoliation, and Justina's opinion of her actually was that if she could be made to believe that she, Justina, had any rights in John Mortimer, she would not stand in her light, even though she might have begun to think highly of his house, and his position, as advantageous for herself. Love she did not take into her consideration, she neither felt that nor imputed it to others.

She was thoroughly mean herself, but if Emily had done anything mean, it would positively have shaken her faith and trust in Goodness itself. It would actually have been bad for her, and there is no saying how much lower she might have declined, if one of the few persons she believed in had made a descent.

Though she thought thus of Emily, she had notwithstanding felt towards her a kind of serene superiority, as might be felt towards one who could only look straight before her, by one who could see round a corner; but that morning, for the first time, she had begun to fear her, to acknowledge a certain charm in her careless, but by no means ungracious indifference; in her sweet, natural ways with John's children, and in those dark lashes which clouded her soft grey eyes.

The contradictions in her face were dangerous; there was a wistful yearning in her smile; joyous as her laugh sounded, she often put a stop to its sudden sweetness with a sigh.

Justina felt Emily's silence very oppressive, and while it lasted she fully expected that it would be broken at last by some important words.

Emily might tell her that she must be deceiving herself, and might be able to give such decisive proof of the fact as would oblige her to give up this new hope. That was what Justina feared. On the other hand, she might show her ignorance and lighten Justina's heart by merely asking her whether she thought she could love and bear with another woman's children. She might even ask whether John Mortimer had made his intentions plain.

But no, when Emily did speak, she appeared completely to ignore these hints, though her face retained its air of wonder and cogitation.

"By-the-bye, Justina," she said, "you put me a little out of countenance just now. John Mortimer never meant to ask us to luncheon; I know he seldom or ever comes home in the middle of the day."

"Are you sure of that?" said Justina.

"Quite sure; you invited yourself."

"Did I make a mistake? Well, if he did not at first intend it, he certainly caught at the notion afterwards."

"Do you think so? I thought, on the contrary, that he spent some moments in considering what day he could spare to come and receive us."

"Perhaps it is just as well," answered Justina; "I should have felt very awkward going about his house and garden in his absence."

"Justina," said Emily, driven at last to front the question, "how much do you wish me to understand?"

"Nothing at all, dear, but what you see," she replied, without lifting her head from her work;

then she added, "Do those children come here often?"

"Two or three times a week, I think," answered Emily, with a degree of carelessness that attracted Miss Fairbairn's attention. She had appeared more than commonly indifferent that morning, she had hardly responded to the loving caresses of John's children, but this had seemed to signify nothing, they came and hung about her just the same.

"They had taken those gardens some time before I found it out," she continued. "They run through the copses and through those three or four fields that belong to John, and get into my garden over the stepping-stones in the brook."

"They must feel very sure of their welcome," said Justina, rather pointedly.

"Yes," answered Emily, also rather pointedly; "but I have never invited them to come, never once; there is, as you see, no occasion."

Holding her graceful head a little higher than usual, she folded up her now finished shawl, ran up-stairs with it to Miss Christie's room, and was conscious almost at once (or she fancied so) that her old aunt looked at her with a certain air of scrutiny, not unmixed with amusement. She was relieved when she had put on her gift to hear Miss Christie say, "Well, ye'll be glad to know that I feel more at my ease now than I've done for some time."

There had been such an air of triumph in Miss Christie's glance that Emily was pleased to find she was only exultant on account of her health. She expressed her gladness, and assured the old lady she would soon be as active as ever.

"It's no my foot I'm thinking of," answered Miss Christie, "but some bad advice that weighed on my mind—bad advice that I've given to John Mortimer." Thereupon she related the conversation in which she had recommended Miss Fairbairn to him.

Emily sat very still—so still, that she hardly seemed to breathe, then, looking up, she said, perhaps rather more calmly and quietly than was her wont—

"Several people have thought it would be a good thing for John to marry Justina Fairbairn."

"And I was one of them," quoth Miss Christie, her eyes sparkling with joy and malice, "but I've thought lately that I was just mistaken," and she presently related what had passed between her and John that morning.

Emily's fair cheek took a slight blush-rose tint. If she felt relieved, this did not appear; perhaps she thought, "Under like circumstances John would speak just so of me." The old lady had been silent some moments before Emily answered, and when she did speak she said—

"What! you and John actually joked about poor Justina in her presence, auntie?"

"Did I see him in her absence?" inquired Miss Christie, excusing herself. "I tell ye, child, I've changed my mind. John Mortimer's a world too good for her. Aye, but he looked grand this morning."

"Yes," answered Emily, "but it is a pity he thinks all the women are in love with him!" Then, feeling that she had been unjust, she corrected herself, "No, I mean that he is so keenly aware how many women there are in the neighbourhood who would gladly marry him."

"Aware!" quoth Miss Christie, instantly taking his part. "Aware, indeed! Can he ever go out, or stop at home, that somebody doesn't try to make him aware! Small blame to them," she added with a laugh, "few men can hold their heads higher, either moreally or pheesically, and he has his pockets full of money besides."

Emily got away from Miss Christie as soon as she could, put on her bonnet, and went into the garden.

The air was soft, and almost oppressively mild, for the bracing east wind was gone, and a tender wooing zephyr was fluttering among the crumbled leaves, and helping them to their expansion. Before she knew what instinct had taken her there, she found herself standing by the four little gardens, listening to the cheerful dance of the water among the stepping-stones, and looking at the small footsteps of the children, which were printed all over their property.

Yes, there was no mistake about that, her empty heart had taken them in with no thought and no fear of anything that might follow.

Only the other day and her thoughts had been as free as air, there was a sorrowful shadow lying behind her; when she chose, she looked back into it, recalled the confiding trust, and marital pride, and instinctive courage of her late husband, and was sufficiently mistress of her past to muse no more on his unopened mind, and petty ambitions, and small range of thought. He was gone to heaven, he could see farther now, and as for these matters, she had hidden them; they were shut down into night and oblivion, with the dust of what had once been a faithful heart.

Fred Walker had been as one short-sighted, who only sees things close at hand, but sees them clearly.

Emily was very long-sighted, but in a vast range of vision are comprehended many things that the keenest eyes cannot wholly define, and some that are confused with their own shadows.

Things near she saw as plainly as he had done, but the wondrous wide distance drew her now and again away from these. The life of to-day would sometimes spend itself in gazing over the life in her whole day. Her life, as she felt it, yearning and passioning, would appear to overflow the little cup of its separation, or take reflections from other lives, till it was hardly all itself, so much as a small part of the great whole, God's immortal child, the wonderful race of mankind, held in the hand of its fashioner, and conscious of some yearning, the ancient yearning towards its source.

Emily moved slowly home again, and felt rather sensitive about the proposed luncheon at John Mortimer's house. She wished she had managed to spare him from being obliged to give the invitation. She even considered whether Justina could be induced to go alone. But there was no engagement that could be pleaded as a reason for absenting herself. What must be done was before they went, to try, without giving needless pain, to place the matter in a truer light. This would only be fair to poor Justina.

Emily scarcely confessed to her own heart that she was glad of what Miss Christie had said. She was not, from any thought that it could make the least difference to herself, but, upon reflection, she felt ashamed of how John Mortimer had been wooed, and of how he had betrayed by his smile that he knew it.

That day was a Tuesday, the luncheon was to take place on Saturday, but on Friday afternoon Emily had not found courage or occasion to speak to her friend. The more she thought about it, the more difficult and ungracious the matter seemed.

Such was the state of things. Miss Christie was still up-stairs, Justina was seated at work in the drawing-room, and Emily, arrayed in a lilac print apron, was planting some fresh ferns in her *jardinière* when the door was opened, and the servant announced Mr. Mortimer. Emily was finishing her horticulture, and was not at all the kind of person to be put out of countenance on being discovered at any occupation that it suited her fancy to be engaged in. She, however, blushed beautifully, just as any other woman might have done, on being discovered in her drawing-room so arrayed, and her hands acquainted with peat.

She presently left the room. John knew she was gone to wash her hands, and hoped she would not stay away long. "For it won't do, my lady," he thought, "however long you leave me. I will not make an offer to the present candidate, that I am determined!"

In the meantime Justina, wishing to say something of Emily that would sound amiable, and yet help her own cause, remarked pleasantly—

"Emily is a dear, careless creature—just like what she was as a girl" (careless creatures, by-the-bye, are not at all suited to be stepmothers).

"Yes," answered John, in an abstracted tone, and as if he was not considering Mrs. Walker's mental characteristics, which was the case, for he was merely occupied in wishing she would return.

"But she wishes to look well, notwithstanding," continued Justina, as if excusing her, "so no wonder she goes to divest herself of her housemaid's apron."

"Ah," said John, who was no great observer of apparel, "I thought she was not dressed as usual;" but he added, "she is so graceful, that in any array she cannot fail to look well."

Justina looked up feeling hurt, and also a little surprised. Here she was, alone with John Mortimer for the first time in her life, and he was entertaining her with the praise of another woman; but she had a great deal of self-command, and she began almost at once to ask him some questions about his children. She had a most excellent governess to recommend, and was it not true that they wanted a nurse also? Yes, Mr. Mortimer did want both, and, as Justina had been writing to every friend she had about these functionaries, and had heard of several, she mentioned in each case the one she thought most suitable, and John, much pleased at the happy chance which brought such treasures before him, was deep in conversation about them when Emily reappeared, and then, to Justina's great annoyance, he took down two addresses, and broke off the conversation with her instantly to say—

"Emily, I am come to make the humblest apologies possible. I find that I am absolutely obliged to go to London to-morrow on a matter that cannot be postponed."

Justina was greatly mortified, but she answered instantly, and not Emily—

"Ah, then of course you are come to put us off, Mr. Mortimer?"

There was no undue stress on the words "put us off," but they suggested an idea to John that was new to him, and he would have felt called upon to act upon them, and renew the invitation, if Emily had not answered just as if she had heard not a syllable.

"We shall be sorry to miss you, John, when we come, but no doubt the children will be at home, and the girls."

"Yes," said John, slipping into this arrangement so easily, that how little he cared about her visit ought to have been at once made plain to Justina.

"Oh yes, and they will be so proud to entertain you. I hope you will honour them, as was intended, by coming to lunch."

"Yes, to be sure," Emily answered with readiness. "I hope the auriculas will not have begun to fade, they are Miss Fairbairn's favourite flower."

Then, to the intense mortification of Justina, John changed the subject, as if it had been one of no moment to him. "I have been over to Wigfield-house this afternoon to pay my respects to Mrs. Brandon and her boy."

"You found them well, I know, for we were there this morning."

"Perfectly well," said John, and he laughed. "Giles was marching about in the garden with that astonishing infant lying flat on his arm, and with its long robes dangling down. Dorothea (come out, I was told, for the first time) was walking beside him, and looking like a girl of sixteen. I believe when I approached they were discussing to what calling in life they would bring up the youngster. I was desired to remark his uncommon likeness to his father; told that he was considered a very fine child, and I should have had the privilege of looking at his little downy black head, but his mother decided not to accord it, lest he should take cold."

"And so you laugh at her maternal folly," said Justina smiling, but not displeased at what sounded like disparagement of an attractive young woman.

"I laugh at it?—yes! but as a man who feels that it is the one lovely folly of the world. Who could bear to think of all that childhood demands of womanhood, if he did not bear in mind the sweet delusive glamour that washes every woman's eyes ere she catches sight of the small mortal sent to be her charge."

Then Justina, who had found a few moments for recovering herself and deciding how to act, took the conversation again into her own hands, and very soon, in spite of Emily, who did not dare to interfere again, John Mortimer was brought quite naturally and inevitably to add to the desire that they would the next day visit his children, an invitation to luncheon after he should have returned.

Justina accepted.

"But it must not be this day week," she observed with quiet complacency, "for that is to be the baby's christening day, and I am asked to be his godmother."

Emily could not forbear to look up; John's face was quite a study. He had just been asked to stand for the child, had consented, and whom he might have for companions he had not thought of asking.

"It will be the first anniversary of their wedding," said Emily by way of saying something, for John's silence began to be awkward.

Mrs. Brandon, having been charmed with the sensible serenity of Miss Fairbairn's conversation, and with the candour and straightforwardness that distinguished her, had cultivated her acquaintance with assiduity, and was at that moment thinking how fortunate she was in her baby's sponsors.

When Justina found that John Mortimer was to be present at this christening, and in such a capacity too, she accomplished the best blush her cheek had worn for years. It was almost like an utterance, so completely did it make her feelings known. As for John, he had very seldom in his life looked as foolish as he did then.

Why had he been asked together with Miss Fairbairn? Whatever he might have thought concerning her, his thought was his own; he had never made it manifest by paying her the least attention. He did not like her now so well as he might have done, if he had not tried and failed to make himself like her more. She was almost the only woman now concerning whom he felt strongly that she would not do for him. Surely people did not think he had any intentions towards her. He sat silent and discomfited till Emily, again quite aware of his feelings, and sure he wanted to go, made the opportunity for him, helped him to take advantage of it, and received a somewhat significant smile of thanks as he departed.

"Emily," exclaimed Justina, as soon as the door was shut, "what can you be thinking of? You almost dismissed Mr. Mortimer! Surely, surely you cannot wish to prevent his coming here to see me."

Justina spoke with a displeasure that she hardly cared to moderate. Emily stood listening till she was sure John Mortimer had left her house, then she said something that was meant to serve for an answer, got away as soon as she could, ran up-stairs, hurried to her own room, and locked the door.

"Not alone!" was her first startled thought, but

it was so instantaneously corrected that it had scarcely time to shape itself into words. The large cheval glass had been moved by her own orders, and as she stood just within the door, it sent back her image to her, reflected from head to foot.

She advanced gazing at herself, at the rich folds of her black silk gown made heavy with crape, and at the frail gossamer she carried on her head, and which, as she came on, let its long appendages float out like pennons in her wake. Emily had such a high, almost fantastic notion of feminine dignity (fantastic because it left too much out of view that woman also is a human creature), that till this day it might almost have been said she had not taken even her own self into her confidence. She hardly believed it, and it seems a pity to tell.

Her eyes flashed with anger, while she advanced, as if they would defy the fair widow coming on in those seemly weeds.

"How dare you blush?" she cried out almost aloud. "Only a year and a fortnight ago kneeling by his coffin—how dare you blush? I scorn you!"

She put her hands to her throat, conscious of that nervous rising which some people call a ball in it;

then she sat down full in view of herself, and felt as if she should choke. She was so new to the powerful fetters that had hold of her, were dragging her on, frightening her, subduing her.

Was she never to do or to be any more what she chose—never to know the rest and sweetness of forgetting even for a little while? Why must she be mastered by a voice that did not care at all whether its cadence and its fall were marked by her or not? Why must she tremble and falter even in her prayer, if a foot came up the aisle that she could not bear to miss, and yet that was treading down, and doomed, if this went on, to tread down all reviving joy, and every springtide flower that was budding in her heart?

"No more to be kept back than the rising of the tide"—these were her words—"but, oh, not foreseen as that is, and not to go down any more."

She almost raged against herself. How could she have come there—how could she, why had she never considered what might occur? Then she shed a few passionate tears. "Is it really true, Justina Fairbairn's would-be rival? And neither of us has the slightest chance in the world. Oh, oh, if anything—

anything that ever was or could be, was able to work a cure, it would be what I have seen twice this week. It would be to watch another woman making a fool of herself to win his favour, and to see him smile and know it. Oh, this is too miserable, far too humiliating. The other day, when he came, I cared so little; to-day I could hardly look him in the face."

Then she considered a little longer, and turned impatiently from her image in the glass.

"Why, I have known him all my life, and never dreamed of such a thing! But for that rainy Sunday three weeks ago, I never might have done. Oh, this must be a mere fancy. While I talked to him I felt that it ought to be—that it was. Yes, it is."

Her eyes wandered over the lawn. She could see the edges of those little gardens. She had looked at them of late more often than was prudent. "Darlings!" she whispered with such a heartsick sigh, "how keenly I loved them for the sake of my little lost treasure, before ever I noticed their beautiful likeness to their father—no, that's a mistake. I say it is—I mean to break away from it. And even if it was none, after the lesson I have had to-day, it must and shall be a mistake for ever."

## CHAPTER XII.

### THAT RAINY SUNDAY.

"He hath put the world in their hearts.'

THIS is how that had come about which was such a trouble and oppression to Emily.

Emily was walking to church on a Sunday morning, just three weeks before John Mortimer's first call upon her.

Her little nephew, Dorothea's child, was four days old. He had spent many of his new-found hours sleeping in her arms, while she cherished him with a keen and painful love, full of sweet anguish and unsatisfied memories.

The tending of this small life, which in some sort was to be a plenishing for her empty heart, had, however, made her more fully alive than usual to the loneliness of her lot, and as she walked on through a fir-wood, in the mild weather, everything seemed also to be more alive, waking, and going to change. The lights that slanted down were more significant. The little shaded hollows were more pathetic, but on the whole it seemed as if the best part of the year was coming on for the world. It made her heart ache to feel or fancy how glad the world was, and how the open sky laughed down upon it in helpful sympathy. The old question presents itself over and over again to be answered,—What is it that gives us so much joy in looking at earth and air and water?

We love a landscape, but not merely because remoteness makes blue the distant hills, as if the sky itself having come down, we could look through a portion of it, as through a veil. It is not the vague possibility of what may be shrouded in the blue that stirs our hearts. We know that if we saw it close it would be set full of villages, and farmhouses, lanes and orchards, and furrowed fields; no other, and not fairer than we have near.

Is it what we impart, or impute to nature from ourselves, that we chiefly lean upon? or does she truly impart of what is really in her to us?

What delight we find in her action, what sentiment

in her rest! What passion we impute to her changes, what apathy of a satisfying calming sort to her decline!

If one of us could go to another world, and be all alone in it, perhaps that world would appear to be washed perfectly clean of all this kind of beauty, though it might in itself and for itself be far more beautiful than ours.

Who has not felt delight in the grand movements of a thunder-storm, when the heavens and earth come together, and have it out, and seem to feel the better for it afterwards, as if they had cleared off old scores? The sight of noble wrath, and vehement action, cannot only nerve the energetic; they can comfort those obliged to be still. There is so little these may do, but the elements are up and doing; and they are in some sort theirs.

And who does not like to watch the stately white cloud lying becalmed over the woods, and waiting in a rapture of rest for a wind to come and float it on? Yet we might not have cared to see the cloud take her rest, but for the sweetness of rest to ourselves. The plough turned over on one side under a hedge, while the ploughman rests at noon, might hint to us what is the key-note of that chord which makes us think the rest of the cloud so fair.

If the splendour of some intense passion had never suddenly glorified the spread-out ether of time in which our spirits float, should we feel such a strange yearning on looking at a sunset, with its tender preliminary flush, and then the rapid suffusions of scarlet and growth of gold? If it is not ourselves that we look at then, it is at one of the tokens and emblems which claim a likeness with us, a link to hold us up to the clear space that washes itself so suddenly in an elixir costly as the golden chances of youth, and the crimson rose of love. With what a sigh, even youth itself will mark that outpouring of coloured glory! It whelms the world and overcomes the sky, and then, while none withstand it, and all is its own, it will change as if wearied, and on a sudden be over; or with pathetic withdrawal faint slowly away.

Her apathy, too—her surrender, when she has had everything, and felt the toil in it, and found the hurry of living. The young seldom perceive the apathy of nature; eyes that are enlightened by age can often see her quiet in the autumn, folding up her best things, as they have done, and getting ready to put them away under the snow. They both expect the spring.

Emily was thinking some such thoughts as these while she walked on to the small country church alone. She went in. This was the first Sunday after the funeral of old Augustus Mortimer. A glance showed her that John was at church, sitting among his children.

The Mortimers were much beloved thereabout. This was not the place where the old man had worshipped, but a kindly feeling towards his son had induced the bringing out of such black drapery as the little church possessed. It was hung round the pulpit, and about the wall at the back of his pew; and as he sat upright, perfectly still, and with his face set into a grave, immobile expression, the dark background appeared to add purity to the fair clear tints of his hair and complexion, and make every line of his features more distinct.

And while she looked from time to time at this face, the same thing occurred to her, as does to us in looking at nature; either she perceived something she had never known of or looked for before, or she imparted to his manhood something from the tenderness of her womanhood, and mourned with him and for him.

For this was what she saw, that in spite of the children about him (all in deep mourning), his two tall young daughters and his sweet little girls and boys, there was a certain air of isolation about him, a sort of unconsciousness of them all as he towered above them, which gave him a somewhat desolate effect of being alone. The light striking down upon his head and the mourning drapery behind him, made every shadow of a change more evident. She knew how the withdrawal of this old father weighed on his heart, and his attitude was so unchanging, and his expression so guarded, that she saw he was keeping watch over his self-possession, and holding it well in hand.

All this appeared so evident to her that she was relieved, as the service went on, to find him still calm and able to command himself, and keep down any expression of trouble and pain. He began to breathe more freely too; but Emily felt that he would not meet any eyes that day, and she looked at him and his children many times.

In the middle of the sermon a dark cloud came

over, and before the service was finished it poured with rain. Emily was not going back to her brother's house; she had only the short distance to traverse that led to her own, and she did not intend to speak to the Mortimers; so she withdrew into the porch, to wait there till they should have passed out by the little door they generally used. They scarcely ever had out a carriage on Sunday, for John preserved many of his father's habits, without, in all cases, holding the opinions which had led to them.

That day, however, the servants brought a carriage, and as the little girls were carried to it under umbrellas they caught sight of Emily, and to her annoyance, she presently saw John advancing to her. She had already begun to walk when he met her, and, sheltering her with his umbrella, proposed to take her home in the carriage; but she declined; she felt the oppression and sadness of his manner, and knew he did not want her company. "I would much rather walk," she declared.

"Would you?" he said, and waved to the men to take the carriage on. "Well, it is not far;" and he proceeded to conduct her. Indeed there was nothing else for him to do, for she could not hold up her umbrella. He gave her his arm, and for two or three minutes the wind and the rain together made her plenty of occupation; but when they got under the shelter of the cliff-like rock near her house she felt the silence oppressive, and thinking that nothing to the purpose, nothing touching on either his thoughts or her own, would be acceptable, she said, by way of saying something,—

"And so Valentine is gone! Has he written from Melcombe to you, John?"

"No," John answered, and added, after another short silence, "I feel the loss of his company; it leaves me the more alone."

Then, to her surprise, he began at once to speak of this much-loved old man, and related two or three little evidences of his kindness and charity that she liked to hear, and that it evidently was a relief to him to tell. She was just the kind of woman unconsciously to draw forth confidences, and to reward them. Something poignant in his feeling was rather set forth than concealed by his sober, self-restrained ways and quiet words; it suited Emily, and she allowed herself to speak with that tender reverence of the dead which came very well from her, since she had loved him living so well. She was rather eloquent when her feelings were touched, and then she had a sweet and penetrative voice. John liked to hear her; he recalled her words when he had parted with her at her own door, and felt that no one else had said anything of his father that was half so much to his mind. It was nearly four weeks after this that Emily fully confessed to herself what had occurred.

The dinner, after John Mortimer withdrew that day and Emily made to herself this confession, was happily relieved by the company of three or four neighbours, otherwise the hostess might have been made to feel very plainly that she had displeased her guest. But the next morning Justina, having had time to consider that Emily must on no account be annoyed, came down all serenity and kindliness. She was so attentive to the lame old aunt, and though the poor lady, being rather in pain, was decidedly snappish, she did not betray any feeling of disapproval.

"Ay," said Miss Christie to herself when the two ladies had set off on their short walk, "yon's not so straightforward and simple as I once thought her. Only give her a chance, and as sure as death she'll get hold of John, after all."

Emily and Justina went across the fields and came to John's garden, over the wooden bridge that spanned the brook.

The sunny sloping garden was full of spring flowers. Vines, not yet in leaf, were trained all over the back of the house, clematis and jasmine, climbing up them and over them, were pouring themselves down again in great twisted strands; windows peeped out of ivy, and the old red-tiled roof, warm and mossy, looked homely and comfortable. A certain air of old-fashioned, easy comfort pervaded the whole place; large bay windows, with little roofs of their own, came boldly forth, and commanded a good view of other windows—ivied windows that retired unaccountably. There were no right lines. Casements at one end of the house showed in three tiers, at the other there were but two. The only thing that was perfectly at ease about itself, and quite clear that it ought to be seen, was the roof. You could not possibly make a "stuck-up" house, or a smart villa, or a modern family house of one that had a roof like that. The late Mrs. Mortimer had wished it could be taken away. She would have liked the house to be higher and the roof lower. John on the other hand, delighted in his roof, and also in his stables, the other remarkable feature of the place.

As the visitors advanced, children's voices greeted them; the little ones were running in and out; they presently met and seized Mrs. Walker, dancing round her, and leading her in triumph into the hall. Then Justina observed a good-sized doll, comfortably put to bed on one of the hall chairs, and tightly tucked up in some manifest pinafores; near it stood a child's wheel-barrow, half full of picture-books. "I shall not allow that sort of litter here when I come, as I hope and trust I soon shall do," thought Justina. "Children's toys are all very well in their proper places."

Then Justina, who had never been inside the house before, easily induced the children to take her from room to room, of those four which were thoroughfares to one another. Her attentive eyes left nothing unnoticed, the fine modern water-colour landscapes on the walls of one, the delicate inlaid cabinets in another. Then a library, with a capital billiard-table, and lastly John's den. There was something about all these rooms which seemed to show the absence of a woman. They were not untidy, but in the drawing-room was John's great microscope, with the green-shaded apparatus for lighting it; the books also from the library had been allowed to overflow into it, and encroach upon all the tables. The dining-room alone was as other people's dining-rooms, but John's own den was so very far gone in originality and strangeness of litter, that Justina felt decidedly uneasy when she saw it; it made manifest to her that her hoped-for spouse was not the manner of man whom she could expect to understand; books also here had accumulated, and stood in rows on chairs and tables and shelves; pipes were lying on the stone chimneypiece, sharing it with certain old and new, beautiful and ugly bronzes; long papers of genealogies and calculations in John's handwriting were pinned against the walls; various broken bits of Etruscan pottery stood on brackets here and there. It seemed to be the owner's habit to pin his lucubrations about the place, for here was a vocabulary of strange old Italian words, with their derivations, there a list of peculiarities and supposed discoveries in an old Norse dialect.

Emily in the meantime had noticed the absence of the twins; it was not till lunch was announced, and she went back into the dining-room that she saw them, and instantly was aware that something was amiss.

Justina advanced to them first, and the two girls, with a shyness very unusual with them, gave her their hands, and managed, but not without difficulty, to escape a kinder salutation.

And then they both came and kissed Emily, and began to do the honours of their father's table. There was something very touching to her in that instinct of good breeding which kept them attentive to Miss Fairbairn, while a sort of wistful sullenness made the rosy lips pout, and their soft grey eyes twinkle now and then with half-formed tears.

Justina exerted herself to please, and Emily sat nearly silent. She saw very plainly that from some cause or other the girls were looking with dread and dislike on Justina as a possible step-mother. The little ones were very joyous, very hospitable and friendly, but nothing could warm the cold shyness of Gladys and Barbara. They could scarcely eat anything; they had nothing to say.

It seemed as if, whatever occurred, Justina was capable of construing it into a good omen. Somebody must have suggested to these girls that their father meant to make her his second wife. What if he had done it himself? Of course, under the circumstances, her intelligence could not fail to interpret aright those downcast eyes, those reluctant answers, and the timid, uncertain manner that showed plainly they were afraid of her. They did not like the notion, of course, of what she hoped was before them. That was nothing; so, as they would not talk, she began to devote herself to the younger children, and with them she got on extremely well.

Emily's heart yearned with a painful pity that returned upon herself over the two girls. She saw in what light they regarded the thought of a stepmother. Her heart ached to think that she had not the remotest chance of ever standing in such a relation towards them. Yet, in despite of that, she was full of tender distress when she considered that if such a blissful possibility could ever draw near, the love of all these children would melt away. The elder ones would resent her presence, and teach the younger to read all the writing of her story the wrong way. They would feel her presence their division from the father whom they loved. They would brood with just that same sullen love and pouting tenderness—they would pity their father just the same, whoever wore his ring, and reigned over them in his stead.

Emily, as she hearkened to Justina's wise and kindly talk, so well considered and suitable for the part she hoped to play—Emily began to pity John herself. She wanted something so much better for him. She reflected that she would gladly be the governess there, as she could not be the wife, if that would save John from throwing himself into matrimony for his children's sake; and yet had she not thought a year ago that Justina was quite good enough for him? Ah, well! but she had not troubled herself then to learn the meaning of his voice, and look so much as once into the depths of his eyes.

Lunch was no sooner over than the children were eager to show the flowers, and all went out. Barbara and Gladys followed, and spoke when appealed to; but they were not able to control their shoulders so well as they did their tongues. Young girls, when reluctant to do any particular thing, often find their shoulders in the way. These useful, and generally graceful, portions of the human frame appear on such occasions to feel a wish to put themselves forward, as if to bear the brunt of it, and their manner is to do this edgeways.

Emily heard Justina invited to see the rabbits and all the other pets, and knew she would do so, and also manage to make the children take her over the whole place, house included. She, however, felt a shrinking from this inspection, an unwonted diffidence and shyness made her almost fancy it would be taking a liberty. Not that John would think so. Oh, no; he would never think about it.

They soon went to look at the flowers; and there was old Swan ready to exhibit and set off their good points.

"And so you had another prize, Nicholas. I congratulate you," remarked Emily.

"Well, yes, ma'am, I had another. I almost felt, if I failed, it would serve me right for trying too often. I said it was not my turn. 'Turn,' said the umpire; 'it's merit we go by, not turn, Mr. Swan,' said he."

"And poor Raby took a prize again, I hear," said Emily. "That man seems to be getting on, Swan."

"He does, ma'am; he's more weak than wicked,

that man is. You can't make him hold up his head; and he's allers contradicting himself. He promised his vote last election to both sides. 'Why,' said I, 'what's the good of that, William? Folks 'll no more pay you for your words when you've eaten them than they will for your bacon.' But that man really couldn't make up his mind which side should bribe him. Still, William Raby is getting on, I'm pleased to say."

Justina had soon seen the flowers enough, and Emily could not make up her mind to inspect anything else. She therefore returned towards the library, and Barbara walked silently beside her.

As she stepped in at the open window, a sound of sobbing startled her. An oil painting, a portrait of John in his boyhood, hung against the wall. Gladys stood with her face leaning against one of the hands that hung down. Emily heard her words distinctly: "Oh, papa! Oh, papa! Oh, my father beloved!" but the instant she caught the sound of footsteps, she darted off like a frightened bird, and fled away without even looking round.

Then the twin sister turned slowly, and looked at Emily with entreating eyes, saying—

"Is it true, Mrs. Walker? Dear Mrs. Walker, is it really true?"

Emily felt cold at heart. How could she tell? John's words went for nothing; Miss Christie might have mistaken them. She did not pretend to misunderstand, but said she did not know; she had no reason to think it was true.

"But everybody says so," sighed Barbara.

"If your father has said nothing—" Emily began.

"No," she answered; her father had said nothing at all; but the mere mention of his name seemed to overcome her.

Emily sat down, talked to her, and tried to soothe her; but she had no distinct denial to give, and in five minutes Barbara, kneeling before her, was sobbing on her bosom, and bemoaning herself as if she would break her heart.

Truly the case of a step-mother is hard.

Emily leaned her cheek upon the young upturned forehead. She faltered a little as she spoke. If her father chose to marry again, had he not a right? If she loved him, surely she wanted him to be— happy.

"But she is a nasty, nasty thing," sobbed Barbara,

with vehement heavings of the chest and broken words, "and—and—I am sure I hate her, and so does Gladys, and so does Johnnie too." Then her voice softened again—"Oh, father, father! I would take such care of the little ones if you wouldn't do it! and we would never, never quarrel with the governesses, or make game of them any more."

Emily drew her yet nearer to herself, and said in the stillest, most matter-of-fact tone—

"Of course you know that you are a very naughty girl, my sweet."

"Yes," said Barbara ruefully.

"And very silly too," she continued; but there was something so tender and caressing in her manner, that the words sounded like anything but a reproof.

"I don't think I am silly," said Barbara.

"Yes, you are, if you are really making yourself miserable about an idle rumour, and nothing more."

"But everybody says it is true. Why, one of Johnnie's schoolfellows, who has some friends near here, told him every one was talking of it."

"Well, my darling," said Emily with a sigh, "but even if it is true, the better you take it, the better it will be for you; and you don't want to make your father miserable?"

"No," said the poor child naïvely; "and we've been so good—so very good—since we heard it. But it is so horrid to have a step-mother! I told you papa had never said anything; but he did say once to Gladys that he felt very lonely now Grand was gone. He said that he felt the loss of mamma."

She dried her eyes and looked up as she said these words, and Emily felt a sharp pang of pity for John. He must be hard set indeed for help and love and satisfying companionship if he was choosing to suppose that he had buried such blessings as these with the wife of his youth.

"Oh!" said Barbara, with a weary sigh, "Johnnie does so hate the thought of it! He wrote us such a furious letter. What was my mother like, dear Mrs. Walker? It's so hard that we cannot remember her."

Emily looked down at Barbara's dark hair and lucid blue-grey eyes, at the narrow face and pleasant rosy mouth.

"Your mother was like you—to look at," she answered.

She felt obliged to put in those qualifying words, for Janie Mortimer had given her face to her young daughter; but the girl's passionate feelings and yearning love, and even, as it seemed, pity for her father and herself, had all come from the other side of the house.

Barbara rose when she heard this, and stood up, as if to be better seen by her who had spoken what she took for such appreciative words, and Emily felt constrained to take the dead mother's part, and say what it was best for her child to hear.

"Barbara, no one would have been less pleased than your mother at your all setting yourselves against this. Write and tell Johnnie so, will you, my dear?"

Barbara looked surprised.

"She was very judicious, very reasonable; it is not on her account at all that you need resent your father's intention—if, indeed, he has such an intention."

"But Johnnie remembers her very well," said Barbara, not at all pleased, "and she was very sweet and very delightful, and that's why he does resent it so much."

"If I am to speak of her as she was, I must say that is a state of feeling she would not have approved of, or even cared about."

"Not cared that father should love some one else!"

The astonishment expressed in the young, childlike face daunted Emily for the moment.

"She would have cared for your welfare. You had better think of her as wishing that her children should always be very dear to their father, as desirous that they should not set themselves against his wishes, and vex and displease him."

"Then I suppose I'd better give you Johnnie's letter," said Barbara, "because he is so angry—quite furious, really." She took out a letter, and put it into Emily's hand. "Will you burn it when you go home? but, Mrs. Walker, will you read it first, because then you'll see that Johnnie does love father —and dear mamma too."

Voices were heard now and steps on the gravel. Barbara took up her eyeglass, and moved forward; then, when she saw Justina, she retreated to Emily's side with a gesture of discomfiture and almost of disgust.

"Any step-mother at all," she continued, "Johnnie says, he hates the thought of; but that one— Oh!"

"What a lesson for me!" thought Emily; and she put the letter in her pocket.

"It's very rude," whispered Barbara; "but you mustn't mind that;" and with a better grace than could have been expected she allowed Justina to kiss her, and the two ladies walked back through the fields, the younger children accompanying them nearly all the way home.

END OF VOL. II.

www.ingramcontent.com/pod-product-compliance
Lightning Source LLC
Chambersburg PA
CBHW032148230426
43672CB00011B/2486